A Lifetime of Lessons from the Parent of a Special Needs Child

A Caretaker's Guide to Disability Management

A Lifetime of Lessons
from the Parent of a
Special Needs Child

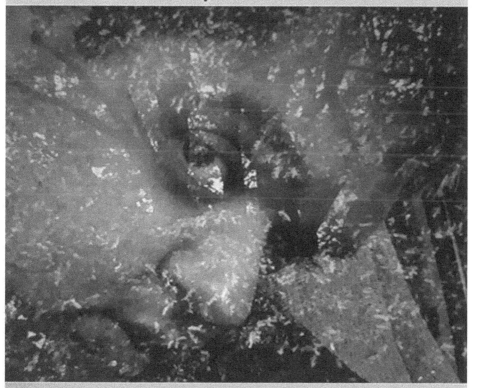

A Caretaker's Guide to Disability Management

Brian A. Wilk

Table of Contents

Introduction

I have been there. I know your fear and heartbreak, your confusion and frustration. I want to help you by affording you the insights and assistance that I didn't have, during what was, unequivocally, the hardest time of my life. I didn't write this book because I wanted to; I wrote it because I *had* to. When you are tasked with being the caretaker of a disabled person, it is a labor of love to be sure, but the harsh reality is that it is also a lifetime of learning hard lessons.

In short, we have been where you are right now with one notable exception: You have this book to use as a reference guide for this life.

This book was written with one goal in mind: to help people who care for disabled persons navigate all the special needs that come with this lifestyle. Presently, there is no book that details the day-to-day struggles that we unique caretakers have to go through, and unless you're living it, you don't *know what we go through*. I will guide you from a perceived sense of hopelessness and bewilderment to a place of confidence and maturity with hindsight of my personal experience and the selfless input of countless people I've encountered during this journey. The lessons learned in this book were gleaned from hundreds of collective years of experience from people who are in your shoes and want to help.

To date, I have lived this lifestyle for twenty-five years and offer suggestions from experience, fact-based solutions, and real-life scenarios. My wife and I have prepared for the possibility of death for our child, sat through three surgeries – one of which literally involved removing the top half of our son's skull, cutting it apart and placing it back together. We have fought through the IEP process with stellar results, taught ourselves to solve complex financial situations involving our son and heirs, and found support groups that have been immensely beneficial to everyone.

This book was fueled by necessity and built by experience and research: Dozens of caretakers who have cared for a wide variety of disabilities were interviewed; schoolteachers, administrators, and professionals were consulted. I took all of that information, condensed it, organized it, and put it into context so you can implement it easily and immediately. I know that you need help and that you need it now (believe me, I know), so I designed this guide to do just that: cover issues from educational conundrums to financial considerations, from family dynamic realties to realistic lifestyle adjustments, and everything in between.

You, as a caretaker, will be empowered to confidently care for your child through any obstacle you will face. Derek taught us that, and I feel obligated to do the same for you. If you've ever wondered "What do I do next?" it's in here, all the way through to adulthood and beyond. My hope is to offer the power of knowledge, experience, and positivity to give you optimism for the best future life for yourselves and your disabled person. My hope is that you enjoy reading this book as much as I have enjoyed writing it.

DISCLAIMER: The medical and financial information found in this book provides helpful and useful information meant to educate the reader. They are my opinions and do not constitute professional advice. As always, seek out a medical professional or financial advisor for your particular situation. The reference

Dedication

Laurie Swanson Wilk with Derek; Dr. Goodrich

I have chosen to dedicate this book to the two most influential people in Derek's life: his mother, Laurie Swanson Wilk, and his neurosurgeon, Dr. James Goodrich. Laurie has dedicated her life to caring, nurturing, and providing the best possible experience for our son. Dr. Goodrich saved his life with his first operation at six months old, and improved it with his second twenty years later. The unselfishness I write about in this book could not have two better examples than these two beautiful souls. A mother's love is something to behold; a mother's special needs love is something special to behold.

Dr. Goodrich, who sadly passed away from COVID-19 during the writing of this book, was the embodiment of unselfishness. As the lead surgeon in a twenty-seven-hour operation separating conjoined Siamese twins at the head, he stepped aside to allow a junior member to make the final cut, symbolically giving life to two persons. The world has lost a great neurosurgeon and an even better person.

Thank you both for your giving nature; Derek and the world have benefitted tremendously from your humanity.

Chapter 1

Laurie and Brian: the Normal Years

"Keep your dreams alive, no matter what. You may have to adjust and be flexible, but above all, keep that dream going."

Brian Wilk

When we first met, my eyes were hypnotized by the most beautiful woman I had ever seen in person. This gorgeous blonde with the porcelain skin, a smile to die for, perfectly applied lipstick, and the inviting light brown eyes lured me in like a siren. I didn't know it at the time, but one day this woman would become my wife. This was the woman who would give me so much love, so much laughter and pleasure, and so much beauty for decades to come. We would couple where others would break apart; we would rise where others would fall; we would persevere where others would fail. She would be the one person I could count on no matter what…. Our lives would be enriched one day with a love like no other, and it wouldn't be the love we shared with one another.

Our wedding song, a minor hit by the band INXS, "Never Tear Us Apart," foreshadowed our lives together. Certainly, there were the normal stressors every marriage encounters that tried to make a liar out of that song, but none were strong enough to accomplish this feat. We clearly have a love that is strong, and I have no doubt that this foundation was vital to us succeeding with Derek, our disabled child. It was already built, this love, and needed less maintenance to stay that way. We didn't have to work on our love; it was already in place and allowed us to focus on our Derek. The only "in excess" we would do was in supporting each other for the cause.

This galvanization set the benchmark for our success with our son and the rest of our family. The unselfishness I often speak of is a great teaching tool to impart to your children. An unselfish person always sees the greater good, the common cause, and is almost always the happiest person in the room. This sense of sharing and caring is strong, and to be empathetic to another's cause will always build an important sense of humanity. It teaches humility. It gives you inclusive insights into life in general and helps you to build your best self.

Not being selfish manifests itself in many areas of life. My pay, the money I earn, is rarely spent on me. It always goes to what is needed at that time for my family. It might be clothes for the kids, a new refrigerator, braces; you get the picture. Other forms include a 401k or IRAs, which are also unselfish. If I contribute to these funds for our family, it provides for a safety net for us and with proper planning, an inheritance for our children.

Being unselfish also means watching out for your mate. *Keep your eyes on the caretaker*; they have a job that weighs heavily on their mind. Be exceptionally aware that any freedoms you can provide for them will be appreciated beyond words. This can come in many forms: take the lead on getting your child dressed, and fed, and to perform the necessary hygiene; tell your spouse to go out with their friends, see a movie, or even just take a drive to clear their mind of stress. Draw your wife a bath, get her some of that takeout food she loves; flowers are never the wrong answer, and poetry never hurts either.

This is what unselfishness looks like. It does the whole clan a whole lot of good. Your spouse feels great being able to get away, she becomes appreciative of what you've done, and you get some bonus one-on-one time with your child. You can do two things with this time: have fun with your little one or be in the moment and understand how difficult this job your spouse does really is, which will help you become even more appreciative yourself.

There are many moments in the lives of our fraternity of people who care for disabled members that make us feel our best days are behind us. There is the ever-present negative emotion of hopelessness that we must embrace and overcome. We feel we ourselves do not have anything to live for, to strive for, and to improve on. The truth is a different story.

This script changes dramatically when we realize where we find ourselves in life; it isn't where we envisioned or what we have experienced. This is exactly what makes this journey epic and challenging. There isn't any road map, there aren't any teachers, and there's no handbook that says this is what I must do. It would be nice to have one, but sarcastically: What fun would that be? I hope to change that with my insights and experience in the following chapters.

Furthermore, the day you had yesterday is not the day you will have today or tomorrow. More often than not, the day changes from morning to mid-morning! Plans are scuttled because of one emergency or another, and it may be an emergency that you have never experienced. The ability to improvise is of the utmost importance. You must keep your wits about you, which is easier said than done.

But a funny thing happens: With each passing crisis that you successfully navigate, you build confidence and strength you never thought you had. You build a better version of yourself and your life. You are continuing to pave the way to building your best possible life. This is satisfying if you allow yourself the opportunity to be satisfied. And you should...the number one reason it is so satisfying is that you did it. You didn't read about it in a book; you experienced the issue, you solved for it, and the solution worked.

Tomorrow may be another learning experience with issues never before encountered, but you have solved for today and that is a good thing. It can never be taken away. It will be the bedrock for future issues, one now stronger because of the confidence you have just gained solving for today's problems. *Caretaking is believing you can do it.*

Once again, take the positive from this situation. Would you be a better self without this challenge of a disabled child? My answer is probably not, and what could possibly be more satisfying than providing a solution to a never-before-experienced problem with no help whatsoever and all by yourself? It's the ultimate test, and one that must be passed as an individual and as part of a team.

Believe you are strong and you will be. You are now officially a problem solver and a vitally important member of your family. Carry yourself high and do not be deterred by the day-to-day events that come your way. You can and will overcome these temporary setbacks just as you've always done. You can do it! *Caretakers stay positive.*

Flexibility: After positivity, this is probably the most important word in the disability vernacular that one must possess. I'm a guy who likes to be free-spirited with a sense of adventure, and I plan for the long term very well. The short term, i.e., daily living, can change on a dime. Plans made at eight a.m. are often scrubbed by nine a.m. I think it is very helpful to keep a couple of thought processes in mind during these trying cancellations and reschedulings.

Almost nothing *has* to be done immediately. Sure, you have to eat three times a day, drink water to survive, and get enough sleep to function properly; however, virtually everything else can be rescheduled or placed in a different order of completion. Read that again. At the end of the day, does it matter if you went outside to get the mail first and then went out to get medication, and then shopped for groceries? Of course it doesn't! Remain flexible in all that you do, and you'll get through the day-to-day struggles much more easily.

Keep your schedule open and malleable. Second, remove the stigma of guilt if something doesn't get done that day. Perfection is unattainable; the pursuit of a better life for all is attainable, but only if you allow yourself a bit of leniency. Be mindful of this at the end of each day; count all the intangible things you possess and dismiss what could have been. Live your life and be content. *Comparison is the thief of joy.*

My wife and I had grandiose plans. You know, those plans that every man who ever met any woman had: a house, children, successful careers, health, and happiness. We dreamt of the day we would travel to Europe, buy the new Cadillac, and the McMansion house, and be able to retire early with sufficient funds for a great retirement. This scenario was clearly within our reach. We had been given the tools by our respective parents to accomplish these achievable goals. Laurie's foundation was rock solid; a great attitude, strong work ethic, and a pedigree of private schooling would have provided the necessary elements for success.

My life was a little bit different, but it provided me with a unique set of skills that included being older than my chrono-logical age as I spent nearly all my childhood with people at least a generation ahead of me in life. I also experienced a certain disturbing turbulence and saw a darker side of life that taught me from the negative side; that's a way to learn as well.

My problem-solving skills and never-say-die attitude were drilled into me like some roughneck in a Texas oilfield. We had the tools; we just needed the experience and time to put them to use. We knew one day, after the children were grown and married, we would be empty nesters, and we wanted to have our fun before that day came. Sometimes, suddenly, like a guardrail getting in the way of a car, plans can change.

We had this wonderful fun, this expectation of happiness every time we were together, so many times; in fact, we were some of the happiest people on the planet. Together we were in our own little sphere, our own blissful, harmonious existence. When I was in the company of this goddess, there was a laser focus, a protective bubble that formed around us, and it was just us two together. Didn't matter if we were at a ballgame with thirty thousand other screaming, maniacal fans; I never saw or heard them. I was focused on my partner, my lover.

At a romantic dinner setting at my apartment, the world stopped about three feet in front of my face. That was where Laurie was, and outside of that bubble, my world ceased to exist. My universe had everything I needed in it. I had never been happier in my life; I had a beautiful girlfriend, so beautiful that I would stop the car for no other reason than to kiss her. Yes, while driving, seemingly out of nowhere, I would just pull my badass 1989 Mustang GT 5.0 to the side of the road and lay one on her. I had to get my fix; it was just that way.

Laurie was a positive, non-judgmental person, with an incredible attitude who was so much fun to be around. We clicked from the outset and just "got" each other. It did not take me long to do the math on this one. I asked for her hand in marriage one year after I met her. It should have been sooner, I know, but have I told you I'm a tad slow on the trigger?

After the presentation of the carbon-rock I gave her while on bended knee, under a bright moonlight sky with a vantage point of downtown Providence, Rhode Island, she said yes. October 11, 1989, was a great night; I got to ask the woman who I thought was the most beautiful woman in the world to marry me, and she said yes! We had our sights set on The Dream, our dream, and the smiles on our faces said so to the rest of the world.

I remember the day I showed my parents the diamond engagement ring I had selected for Laurie. It was as beautiful as she was, with a brilliance emanating from within, and with a little mystery thrown in for good measure. It was Laurie. The old man was impressed and my mom loved it. Laurie would have loved a ring from a bubblegum machine if that's what I had chosen. And that's why I was going to ask her to marry me; material things meant very little to Laurie in terms of friendship and love. She already knew what the important, intangible things in life were. And one other mention; Laurie never threw her beauty in anyone's face. Ask anyone; she is a beautiful woman and my so-called friends are fond of telling me that I out-kicked the coverage with this one! She was grounded, and I was ecstatic to be grounded with her.

The night I asked her didn't go exactly as planned; I was real good friends with everyone in my apartment building including the landlords, who were the owners of the mini-mansion I resided in. I had this cozy tiny basement apartment that was perfect for my time of transition from single guy to married guy.

So the big day came, and I let everyone know that I was asking the love of my life for her hand in marriage. I told them where we'd be going, how I was going to do it, and when we'd be back. So far so good...well, not exactly. The restaurant I took her to, a little spot called Olerio's, was perfect. Romantic, dimly lit, not too busy, just a real good setup for a guy to ask his girl the question. This thing called timing never arrived. I never asked her at the meal like I had said I would to my apartment-dwelling friends.

It's okay; I had a backup plan (I always have a backup plan): I'd ask her at the apartment. Simple enough, comfortable place, I'd get it done there. I'm seeing this in my head, the setting, the ask, the response...we get to the apartment and being the gentleman that I am I opened the door for my lady and that's just when it started to unravel; my awesome friends had decorated my apartment with congratulatory balloons, phrases, banners, and general festivities! They were so thorough they even had the fish in my aquarium wishing us congratulations. So I quickly closed the door, and we ambled back outside into the cool October night to see the Providence skyline at the back of the mansion grounds, which is where the question was asked.

Luckily for me, Laurie had indeed said yes. Life was going to be great; I got to kiss a beautiful woman every day for the rest of my life. I'd work hard, provide for her, grow as a family, save for retirement, and along the way, enjoy her company on vacations we'd take. We'd have an espresso in Florence, enjoy a baguette in Paris, pick a tulip in Holland, and enjoy a glass of wine in Madrid. I'd fulfill my promise of taking her to Hawaii and sit with her, on our plaid couch with the plastic covers at home, in our old age and enjoy the pictures we had taken. We'd talk about the grandkids we had and how fortunate we were to have lived this life. I'd still kiss her good night and tell her I loved her.

Plans. I had 'em. I always have plans.

We stayed child-free by design for a couple of blissful years, enjoyed our time together with date nights out, and dreamed of the life we would have together. We would soon learn that we indeed would have to learn how to be flexible. It takes commitment, a willing spirit, and two people who are willing to give of themselves so that a third may benefit – the very definition of unselfishness. Our dreams and our plans would change dramatically, and we would have to change with them. We would soon learn the meaning of the phrase *expect the unexpected*....

Chapter 2

Our Families and Upbringing/Where We Came From

"To me, family is everything. As a matter of fact, nothing comes close."

Brian Wilk

Laurie came from good stock, born of a handsome Swede named Eric and a French beauty named Marie Lorraine. He was tall, thin, and blue-eyed, with an ever-present smile, his wispy blond hair falling around his collar. He was affable, well-liked, a gentle soul who worked hard and made his family his first priority. If you could build a man from a spec sheet, Eric would be the template. He was impossible not to like and not to try to emulate. The standard line of "men wanted to be him and woman wanted to be with him" was applicable to Eric. He served his country proudly as a Marine.

Lorraine, as she liked to be known, steered the ship and made sure the children were brought up with sound fundamentals and with manners and ethics. She too was kind, considerate, and a mother first. In the days that Eric courted her, she looked remarkably like Audrey Hepburn. When I saw the pictures of them back in their day, I knew why Eric asked her to be his wife. Laurie also had a sister four years her senior, named Linda. Their surname was Swanson, and they carried on the family name with grace and style, and exuded a wonderful serenity and calmness that all could see. Their family was tight. Laurie had lived the family dream already.

Her support system included her parents, her grandparents, and a cul-de-sac type geographic location that came stocked with many children in her age group. They are all still friends with her to this day. They would play manhunt for hours and hours, and her house became the focal point as it was located centrally in the neighborhood.

Her father was that guy, the nicest man you'd ever want to meet. All the neighborhood kids adored him as did his daughters. Laurie and her dad had a special relationship, one that every daughter should have with her father. A touching example of that is when Laurie would wait for her dad at the entrance to the cul-de-sac to come home from his day working at the water company. Eric would stop his pickup truck on the corner, and Laurie would climb in and steer the vehicle the rest of the way home sitting right by her dad.

The distance traveled was probably on the order of three hundred feet or so, but it must have seemed like forever to a child sitting next to her hero. Time must have stood still for Laurie when she was with her dad like it did for me when I was with her. When she first told me this story shortly after we met, you could easily tell it meant the world to her and her dad.

Unfortunately, not long after we started dating, her dad got very sick. He had valiantly fought a cancer scare before I had met Laurie and had temporarily recovered. I was lucky to be able to spend time with Eric, as the job I had at the time, delivering snack chips, took me near his home nearly every day. I would stop in from time to time to check in on him, and I got to know him very well during that time. This time spent together grows more valuable to me the older I get. We talked about baseball, college football (I was a huge Miami Hurricanes fan), and who would win, who would cover, and how much I was willing to bet on those games.

The most important thing by far for me was receiving Eric's permission for his daughter's hand in marriage. You see, I'm very old-fashioned in that sense. If it's protocol and has any-thing to do with romance, I must do it the correct way. Quite frankly, given his condition, no one was sure Eric would make it to the ceremony. Unfortunately, his cancer returned and would eventually take Eric, robbing him of the opportunity to give away his daughter.

To see a man in the prime of his life (Eric was forty-nine when he passed) perish from a silent disease is traumatic on so many levels. This was very difficult on Laurie; she had just lost the most important man in her life. Perhaps, looking back, this time Laurie and I spent together engaging in empathy and developing our bond was another teaching moment for us.

Tragically, I was multi-tasking through her father's situation and my own. My paternal grandfather was also dying of bone cancer. I witnessed two different perspectives on how families cope with death. Each family had a different strategy for their coping mechanisms, and neither was wrong or right. They were correct for each grieving family, and that is exactly how it should be: what works best given the current situation.

Mr. Swanson left behind three beautiful women, with no man to take his place. It was the saddest time of my life to that point. I was able to spend quite a bit of time with their family, and this experience taught me many hard but wonderful lessons. Alas, this moment would define Laurie and me in ways we didn't know yet. The 13th and 15th of December 1989 are two dates we will never forget. My grandfather Anthony passed on the 13th, and Eric passed on the 15th, both from bone cancer. Christmas was absent of spirit that year.

We survived the emotions of loss, grief, shock, and surprise, and at that point, the question one must ask of themselves is "how will you let this define you?" Will you let this bring you down to the depths of despair and depression, or will you learn from this in a way that is positive and uplifting, and that provides for a certain perspective? Will you lament the fact that Eric passed at forty-nine years of age and give up all hope of making it that far yourself, or will you see this tragic event for what it is: a wake-up call about life? The fact is that life is finite; it does have a beginning, a middle, and an end.

Let's examine the first part a little closer. It's easy to start life with happiness. Everything is roses and balloons and big colorful rainbows. It's the refreshing cool sprinkler on a hot and humid summer day, it's the echo of laughter with your friends, and it's the lack of prejudice that has yet to enter your heart. It's the middle and end that bring surprises and obstacles to overcome. This is stuff that blindsides you, stuff that cannot be foreseen by a six-year-old blonde little girl in a cul-de-sac, playing in a puddle, mud caked on her bright yellow dress and wearing maroon shoes.

My story is a tad more complicated, but the message is the same: Take the positives, be optimistic, and keep striving to be the best you can be. I was born in 1961 to working-class parents and would soon be joined by my little brother, Chris, twenty months later. My mother came from the same stock as Eric and Lorraine, just good, law-abiding, conscientious people who wanted to be happy with their families. My mom, Elinor M. Trombley, was my rock, my sage, and my main source of unbelievably good advice. I cannot recall ever being steered the wrong way by her. She would always be proved correct in her advice.

The person everyone else called Ellie was a wonderful woman. She was beautiful in so many ways, and the old saying that you marry your mother is the best homage I can give to my wife. There is no one on the planet I respect more than my mom. Yes, it's said in the present tense, because she is still teaching me to this day, even though she passed away in 2004.

They say you can remember back to about four or five years of age. I can attest to that as one of my fondest memories of my mom was my first day of kindergarten. I cried like a baby, I did not want to leave my mom, and I remember with extreme clarity how scared I was to not be under her loving umbrella. I was honestly petrified, with tears streaming down my face.

Ten minutes after she left I was happy as a clam, making friends and building different shapes with my newfound friends with the large red-paper bricks that were available. I'm not lying when I tell you I do not have another memory that I can recall from my first year in school; I remember that scene vividly, though. I recall the teacher telling my mom that at the end of class I was the only one who put the bricks back where they came from. My mom's smile gave me all the reassurance I ever needed.

All these lessons would come back to help me many years later, about thirty years or so, when Ellie was diagnosed with early onset Alzheimer's. *At age fifty-two.* The call I received from my father was disconcerting, not real, can't be happening, but it was real. I went numb. My brother and I flew down to see mom in Florida, and it was surreal, knowing our mother would not recover from this, knowing time was ticking, and knowing there would be an incredibly difficult road ahead for both her and the family. I remember mom saying, "They're going to see what they can do for me, you know, different medicines…" As her voice trailed off, I knew this would be the last day I would see the mom I had known since kindergarten. I'd see her in her physical form again, of course, but that person blankly staring back at me would be an unrecognizable entity of a woman I loved with all my heart. Not my best day on this planet...

Ellie's disease advanced through the years, and it was a text-book case of early onset Alzheimer's. The memory slowly fades and the family is left to bear witness to a person they do not know. This shell of a person who has regressed to a childlike quality and who will continue to regress until normal everyday functions become impossible is difficult to comprehend. Additionally, there is this "sun downing" effect that all must acknowledge; at the time of sunset, for reasons still not completely understood, a worsening of memory, equilibrium, and the understanding of time and space occur. It is frightening to see the first time and is a cruel reminder of what this disease is about to bring.

And bring it, it does.

The irony of my mom's situation was not lost on me it's ; the hell the family grows through versus the relative ignorance of the person going through this horrid disease. The disease bearers are pretty much clueless as to their pain, while the loved ones are left to wonder what and why is this happening to our mom, our loved one? This dynamic is unique to the grieving friends and relatives of Alzheimer's patients.

Two instances stand out in my thoughts from my early recollec-tion of what prompted me to think something might be amiss with Ms. Ellie. Rhode Island is, of course, a small state, and the main traffic artery that runs through the middle is Route 95. One fine summer day, I was riding shotgun with my mother driving, windows down, radio playing, and we came up to an interchange that led to Route 95. She must have traveled this very same interchange a thousand times in her life, maybe more. Still, she looked at the enormous green traffic sign and said "Which way do I go?" I'm sure I said something like "Ma, go north; what's a matter with you." She chuckled (mom had a great laugh with a bit of a cackle), and we made it home without any other drama.

The second instance is as humorous as it is tragic. Mom being mom asked me if there was anything she could do to make Christmas easier for me. Did I mention I learned unselfishness from this lady? My parents were up for the holidays, and I put my mom to work! I asked her to please wrap all of Laurie's gifts as I hadn't gotten to that yet. This was right up mom's alley as she loved to be creative. Laurie would surely know I hadn't wrapped the presents she was about to open; they would be wrapped too nicely.

Christmas Eve with all its spirit arrived, and tradition at the Wilk estate dictates we open gifts at that time. Well, my brother got himself some lingerie, and my sister-in-law received some of Laurie's favorite perfume! I was looking at my mom and saying "Ma, what the hell happened?" Again, she laughed it off, and I didn't do my best detective work that night; otherwise, I would have known this was the starting point of her disease.

This brings me to the genesis of a crossroads of innocence, disbelief, and an unwilling ability to see the obvious; this woman I've known all my life, a person I know better than any other, and I still refuse to believe what just occurred. It's so hard to accept any disability; it doesn't matter which one. It's the point of normalcy; it's comfortable. It's cream with your coffee on a Sunday morning, it's your side of the bed, and it's your favorite pair of jeans. What is uncomfortable is anything that interferes with your perception of what happens every day.

Mothers forgetting what you just told them is not normal. *This is a feeling we have to learn to embrace as caretakers of a disabled child.*

It's the excuses, I surmise, that make us believe what we want to; hey, mom isn't getting any younger, maybe she's been a little stressed, you know she's not sleeping well.... No one wants to believe the truth, no one. It's frightening, unknown, potentially devastating, and who wants to deal with that? Denial is such a petulant word, but with it comes enormous casualty for the victims involved in any disability.

Success comes to those who identify the issue/problem, gain valuable information, and react to it in a way that supports a healthy environment for all involved. Commitment and an unrelenting spirit of being that indomitable force will ensure complacency never shows its face in your house. *As caretakers, we owe it to our loved ones to see that this takes place.*

As with most tragedies in life, lessons can be gleaned from these landmarks and signposts, lessons that define our character, build our definition of life, and shape our attitudes about what is important. My mother was a young fifty-two years old when she was diagnosed with early onset Alzheimer's. As I stroll through life and open my eyes to more experiences, one of the things I think about often is those unfortunate souls who perish at the doorstep of retirement. Our society requires that its workers labor for about forty to fifty years to pay their penance for a semi-comfortable retirement. We can debate all day long if this is fair or not. Cherish your youth, as retirement is not guaranteed for anyone.

The point I'm trying to drive home is that you can see the sunset, you can smell the roses, and reap the rewards of your life of labor in your sixties in most cases. To have your life taken from you when your dreams will soon be realized may be the cruelest of all fates. We all work for ourselves, and in the broader sense want to leave a legacy of memories and values for our children, some type of inheritance that will make their lives a little easier. Our enjoyment is what we most dream of in our later years, and my heart truly goes out to those persons and families who lose a loved one before they can enjoy the fruits of their labor.

I often think of what my mom would be doing in retirement. She loved to cruise, and no doubt would have had a bucket list of fabulous islands she needed to visit. I can see her on a magnificent ocean liner lying out in all her splendor, getting her fill of ultraviolet rays, wearing oversized sunglasses with a large gaudy straw hat, and having a smile for everyone she meets. Yes, Ms. Ellie would have the requisite umbrella drink in her hand, and you'd hear that cackle, that laugh that let you know Elinor was on that ship.

Mom had style, and on the dance floor she would have been at night, probably elegantly moving to a song by one of her favorites – Engelbert Humperdinck or Barry White. I can still hear those two singing out of the speakers at our house on Waterman Street in Pawtucket when I was a child.

She also loved children, and the love Derek would have received from my mom is something that he or I will never know. She would have embraced him, held him close to her bosom, and nurtured Derek with a song or a lullaby. It's okay, though; mom taught me that too and I do my best to do "what mom would have done." Thanks, mom.

My mother, along with my father, operated a succession of increasingly successful restaurants in the Rhode Island/ Massachusetts market. It's where I cut my teeth, as a twelve-year-old being roused from his bed by a father at 4:30 a.m. Good morning it wasn't! Three hours before school every day, my ass was up working, but wait. There's more. Friday was fish 'n chips day, so I had to come back for three hours after school. We also opened on Saturday from 6 a.m. to 2 p.m. I was there then too. In between, Friday nights were my salvation. I would go to a place called Bobby's Rollaway and roller skate until 11 p.m. or so. I have no idea how I could get up on Saturday mornings to work. Youth can be a wonderful thing.

I can tell you with brutal honesty I hated working all those hours and hated working with my father. He was the epitome of a dominating, no excuses, belittling boss, and those traits spilled over into his parenting style. I was diagnosed with an ulcer at age twelve as I kept everything inside of me, not wanting to confront my father for fear of retribution. It was training camp for my life, one that had yet to be lived. It instilled in me a work ethic that was as big a part of me as any other trait I have, good or bad. I learned what to do and what not to do at an early age.

I grew up fast and started living as an adult way too early. Perhaps it was a blessing in disguise, as I was always looking to balance short-term and long-term goals as a pre-teen. It's just another trait that is needed for a successful marriage and in raising a successful family with a disabled child. I happen to have ownership of this particular trait, and my wife owns many other traits I could not hold a candle to. It's what is clearly needed to be successful in this type of family dynamic.

Let's talk about the glove that holds my hand. Laurie and I fit. She is probably the best parent I have encountered, given all the curveballs life had thrown at her. Let's start with my son from a previous marriage whom Laurie accepted and cared for from the very beginning. Ryan served as our ring bearer for our wedding and he stole the show, looking dapper in his tuxedo and slicked-back blond hair. She treated him as one of her own before we were married, just another reason for me to ask her to get hitched.

When Laurie and I received the news that we would be parents, it was a fantastic day indeed. She did all the right things caring for our little treasure-to-be: eating right, taking her vitamins, and getting plenty of rest. When Ms. Haley made her debut, Laurie was a natural. She really took to being a mother, and we welcomed the first girl in the Wilk family in quite some time. My father was an only child, and of course he had two sons, so having a different chromosome makeup was welcomed whole-heartedly in our family. We didn't know this at the time but little Ms. Haley would be a near replica of my mother in so many ways. Please check out the pics of them both at roughly the same age.

Chapter 3

New Realities and a New Acceptance

"Acceptance of change signifies acceptance of self and a greater understanding of the world in which we reside."

Brian Wilk

Perfectly imperfect: It's a little saying I've given to our lives. We have all been given a life, each one of us. Some of us have beautiful bodies, some have beautiful minds, others have talents for music or singing. Still others possess athletic ability, or the powerful insights to be an artist in any of about a thousand different mediums.

The families who have jurisdiction over a disabled child, those of us who own that responsibility sometimes daydream about what it would be like to have one of the attributes listed above. Maybe even all of them...truth be told, each musician dreams of having an athlete's body. Each singer wishes he could paint his own Mona Lisa, and every model wishes for the ability to write sonnets like Shakespeare.

We are all here in our own body, in our own space at our own time, living with others who we interact with on a daily basis. Everybody has their peaks and valleys, their secret wishes and dreams, but we all are who we are, no more, no less. Our world, our society, and our families need it to be exactly that way; otherwise, how boring and dreadful would life be if we could all dunk a basketball equally well, if we could cite Shakespeare from memory, or light up a canvas with bursting colors that provoke a different imagery for each of us?

The listed attributes would hold no special meaning, no differentiation, nothing to make Chris stand apart from Jen. This
separation allows us our own fingerprint, our own uniqueness
to thrive and survive in this world with a little panache, a little
élan, some flair for the taking. *It is the same way for our
disabled children.*

We are the guardians of their souls, the lamplighters for their
pathways, the guardrails for their journey. We must seek out
what makes these beautiful, adorable, unique children special.
What makes them stand out, what attribute must we recognize
and discover from their bodies and minds? It is up to us to be
the facilitator and nurture what makes them special. And that is
what we call love; in our household, it is Derek's love.

It's these little everyday nuances that bring to light what it
means to be accepting and what it means to accept your new
life. The things all parents dream of for their children, like
hitting a homerun in the bottom of the ninth or being named
class valedictorian, are now put on hold. The actual act is not
going to happen, but it is important to keep the dream alive.
You can't control the homerun not taking place; however, you
can control your response and your dream to the act that your
disabled child *will* be able to do.

I remember something so simple happening to Derek when he
was a toddler. For weeks on end, I had been trying to toilet-
train him. He had the number one down to a science, but
number two was eluding him. I'd sit him on the toilet hoping for
the deuce to appear, but my hopes were dashed time and
again. I never gave up on him, never said this will never happen;
I just kept trying.

One Saturday while he was King of the Throne, it happened! Hallelujah, my son just learned how to do number two. This is not usually cause for front page news in any town or household for that matter. In our house, on that Saturday, though, Derek hit his homerun and Dad cheered, Mom cheered, and history was made at the Wilk domicile. I was never more excited in my life than to see that proud piece of work Derek had accomplished. My other two children have accomplished many feats that I am proud of and have witnessed, and I cheered and attested to their homeruns. I have celebrated all of these accomplishments equally, and I was just as proud of them as I am of Derek.

Here's the reason why. There was a lot of hard work and dedication allotted towards each of their goals. All three had to overachieve to get there, and all three were rewarded as was I. Put another way: What percentage of their potential did each use to get the job done? It was just as hard for Derek to meet his mission as it was for Ryan and Haley to meet theirs.

My reaction is of note here too. I was openly pulling for Derek to get the job done. I did not give up on him nor did I give up on any of my kids' dreams. I celebrated with him knowing that this would be a milestone for him and me. I had three dreams for my children, and all three have been fulfilled. For my son Ryan, I wanted to be the dad who jumped up and cheered when he hit the game-winning homerun in the bottom of the ninth (it was a bunt, close enough!). For my daughter Haley, I wanted her to get a college degree. For Derek, my dream for him has been altered to fit his condition. *Cheerlead for your children, especially those who need it most.*

Derek loves to go for a ride in the car or to watch *Wheel of Fortune*. There are many days I come home, and before I get a step inside the house, he has the picture of a car in his hand. Except in his language it's pronounced "cwah." There are also many days I come home, and I don't feel like going back out, but then there's that thing that he does that makes me reconsider and consent to his wishes. When I put his shoes and jacket on, he jumps up, so excited, with that wild-eyed look, like the look you get when your team scores the winning touchdown, and he kisses me on the lips. It is then that I know why I take him for a ride; it means more to him than my minor inconvenience of resting means to me. My son, teaching me about life yet again! *As caretakers, we must continue to learn and embrace change.*

On our rides in the cwah, it's about family time as Laurie and I get to talk in a relatively controlled environment. Derek is safe in the backseat, seatbelt in place, and doing his rocking motion back and forth that most of the time lets us know that he is happy. If he's having a bad day, we stay close to home in case we have to administer meds. If he's having a good day, we venture out a bit. Flexibility: We use it all the time.

We don't go anywhere special, just a ride down country roads, and I like to take a different route each time to avoid complacency. We usually go around dusk or a little earlier as that's when the animals are out. Living in the country affords the opportunity to view deer, turkeys, foxes, and even the occasional beaver in the many ponds we pass by. It's a therapeutic and relaxing end of the day for all involved.

This is but one type of activity a family with a disabled child/ adult can participate in safely and with a little flexibility built in just in case the journey goes south a bit. Use your imagination and engage your child in these types of activities.

Some examples are going for a walk, setting up a local picnic, eating outside in your own backyard, visiting a coffee shop nearby, or instead of playing Monopoly, creating a game for your child such as throwing a ball in a series of boxes.

The point is to involve all as a family unit. Nearly all activities, with a bit of modification, can be transformed into a useful, happy event for everyone. If you take the time to structure the event this way, the whole family is more apt to participate. A fun time can be had by all, the disabled child was involved, and that should be the end goal.

Derek doesn't talk much; he uses his picture book to communicate. However, he does have a little secret. Don't tell anyone, but my son has a girlfriend. *Wheel of Fortune*'s Vanna White and Derek are an item. When his show comes on, he is king of the letter board. He's calling out Ts, Ss, and Rs like there is no tomorrow, engaged in this show kind of like his father is engaged in the next show, *Jeopardy!*

Time stands still for Derek as he watches and participates in his show, breaking the mundane and the monotony out of his life for thirty minutes. It is wonderful to witness and there are certain sure things in life: death, taxes, and *Wheel of Fortune* being on the TV at the Wilk estate Monday through Saturday at seven p.m. (I tell Derek he lives in an estate; he is, after all, the king of his castle.)

The message here is pretty clear: Take whatever life throws at you and turn those moments of what might otherwise be dreaded into something that benefits your child. It can be real hard work to remain unselfish. *Do it anyway.*

The prize isn't always evident or right at the forefront. What helps me through those doubtful moments is the long-term approach I have to life. I have a job to do, and it's not too complicated at all. My family depends on me to earn the money required to have a decent life and to protect them at all costs.

I'm also charged with keeping them happy and fulfilled. It's in this message that I find solace. It's in this message I find my calling. Some days are difficult; trust me, I get it. But every single day that passes is another success I can look back on for encouragement. I made it all those days precisely *because* of my family, as I know they appreciate everything I do for them. Those special days include the days I come home after a horrendous week at work, and my wife has done my chores or prepared my favorite meal. Those memories are a bank I draw interest on and redeposit when needed in my life's account.

There are other ways to accomplish the same goal. Some people use humor to deflect the ugliness in the world they find themselves in. My take on this is the use of sarcasm and self-deprecation. I use heavy doses of both to get myself and my family through the dark stuff.

Others use therapy, which I highly recommend. I'm a pretty strong person mentally, but sometimes those fights are so daunting that you need a specialist to re-ground your emotions and center you once again for the next day, week, and month. Another possibility is some type of faith, which my wife subscribes to. Doesn't really matter which faith; whichever is comfortable for you and fits your lifestyle is the best probable choice.

Always remember this: You are of little use to fix the situation of a child with a disability if you yourself are broken. Tell me how you can help fix a broken anything, efficiently and proficiently, when you and your emotional self need fixing. If you find yourself questioning if you need help, it's probably time for that help. You owe it to your family and yourself to be on point as we all live in a higher-stress environment than most other families. It doesn't make us any better or worse, just different. And a difference is what you want to make with your family, so get yourself the help you need. You'll get to under-stand how you tick, and with each visit you'll gain more insights and more confidence.

I cannot stress the importance of finding time for what you like to do at least weekly, more if the week isn't going your way. Find that niche enjoyment that puts a smile on your face or a laugh in your conversation and do that, whatever it is. When my day gets crazy, I simply think of others who are not as fortunate as me and cut off the pity party right then and there. Other days my personal enjoyment may come from a hike in the woods, writing a little poetry, or supporting my wife.

Let's go back to those dreams I once had, like the fantasies of traveling with my wife before and after our children were with us. Those dreams must not be written off wholly. I promised my wife I would take her to Hawaii one day. Ironically, the company I worked for had a contest where the top prize was a trip to Hawaii, but alas, I never won.

Spouses can promise their significant others things that may or may not come to pass all the time. I like to keep my promises. Will we ever be going to the Promised Land (Hawaii)? Probably not is the most likely answer, but this doesn't mean my fantasy cannot be altered to fit our current situation.

We recently purchased an RV, and if I could fit it with some of those sea pontoons you see on Amazon, maybe we could get to Hawaii in a couple of weeks. In reality, we will take our "Hawaii" trip via the contiguous forty-eight states. We will take Derek with us and still have fun. We will make the best of the situation, no matter what. Will I hang-glide or parasail or walk the black sand beaches that I visualized in my mind? The answer is no, but I will visit Mt. Rushmore, I will see to it that Laurie fulfills one of her fantasies of an archeological dig, and I will see to it that Derek experiences the best things in life given our collective limitations. I will make it work for all. *It's what caretakers do.*

"Comparison is the Thief of Joy." Truer words may never have been spoken. Do not allow yourself to be caught in this trap. You will live a sordid, non-productive, what if, shallow existence if you do. Be happy for other people in the same way you would be happy for yourself if you bought a new car, went on a trip, or received a promotion. You would want others to be happy for you too, return the favor.

If Joe Blow across the street comes home in a brand new Corvette, be happy. If he and his wife go away for the weekend, be happy. If Jane next door goes on her third cruise this year, without the kids, be happy. You cannot control what another person does, nor should you want to. You can control what you can do and that is to live to the best of your ability given the cards that have been dealt to you. I am genuinely happy for others when they do well. I do not care what they think of me one way or the other. I live my life with my tribe and good or bad, they are all in it with me. This is the cohesiveness that keeps us all together and all on the same plane.

The takeaway here is pretty apparent: Live and love the life you've been given. Life is always about trying to make the best of everything. If you're given a job to do at work, do it the best way you know how. Folding the laundry, doing the dishes, preparing dinner – do it like you're a tenth-degree Black belt in Karate.

You cannot control what is outside of your four walls. Do not be envious of others and always, always be grateful for what is inside of those same four walls. The mindset you create as a caretaker will help you on your trek with your disabled child. Be the force in your life that drives the message home.

Chapter 4

Materialism

"There is no value in life except what you choose to place upon it and no happiness in any place except what you bring to it yourself."

Henry David Thoreau

I'd like to take a moment to talk about materialism. Who is reading this right now who wouldn't like to wear the best dress or tailored suit, drive the best car, and bask in the essence of the best perfumes in the world? Is the dream of accessing all these accoutrements in life really where you want to be? If it is, good for you; you're not harming anyone and you are playing your hand to the best of your ability.

Symbolically, I'll admire you as you walk by, taking in the scent of your Chanel No. 5, while you wear Prada and gaze as you step into your Ferrari. I will live vicariously through you just as I admire the advertisements I watch, I read, and I hear come to life right in front of me.

I will be you for that fleeting moment in time. I will then return to my torn Lee's jeans, the same pair that has the stain on them from when my son decided to spit out his Pringles. Out of necessity, I will drive my 13-year-old Pacifica with the leak in the passenger door that allows rain to enter, that same car that needs a quart of oil every two thousand miles.

I will wear as my perfume sweat and spilled vegetables, along with whatever drink happens to find its way onto my Walmart-bought flannel shirt. And I'll be smiling all the time, knowing I have made a difference in a child's life, glad that Derek is mine and that I am able to provide him a good home with a tremendous amount of support and love in it. That I am married to a woman who is an awesome mother, and a great partner, and that she shares the same values as I do.

In the future, there will be a day when I sit in my rocking chair, old, wrinkled, and wise, blowing concentric circles of smoke towards the ceiling from my cigar, and look back on my greatest accomplishments; nowhere will there be that I made a boatload of money, nowhere will there be I was the best damn salesman ever, nowhere will there be an inkling that I did something that doesn't ultimately matter.

At that moment, it will occur to me that I did the best I could with the cards that were dealt to me. I played the crap out of that hand. I won because my family won, I won because my children won, and I won precisely because I can remember these things that I did. That Ferrari that I didn't own? I drove that ride a thousand times in my dreams; I was faster than Jackie Stewart at Le Mans, quicker than Michael Schumacher at Nürburgring, and quicker still to point out that I never owned that car. And I didn't have to pay four hundred thousand dollars for it either, and I drove it with the options I wanted and in the color I chose, only to give it back at the end of my dream, unscratched and in the same condition I took it out in.

I took what was given to me and stayed positive along the way; I rode the wave, and when the current turned against me, I fought where I could and went where it took me if that was the best option. Fittingly, I always weighed what was best for my family rather than what was best for me. They depended on me, and I can always say I did the right thing by them, and that is why I am happier today than I've ever been. The credits I earned in my lifetime were used to further the interests of my family, my wife, and my children, especially Derek. I have earned my degree in life. *I aspire to be the best caretaker I can be.*

Let's expand for a bit on the divorce rate for autistic families. Fully eighty percent end up in divorce, and this tragedy forever alters the lives of the participants. Here is one couple's scenario: Let's take mom first. She loses the most initially as she cannot work and care for her child at the same time. This means she is probably going to end up on some form of public assistance and the pressure of caring for her child is now magnified immeasurably.

Her mindset is one of hopelessness: "Why, and what the hell do I do now?" Depression sets in. She's had a tough go of it already with two parents helping out. What new battles must she face as a now single parent? The road she has traveled with a partner has now gotten rockier and steeper. She most likely will become bitter, estranged from life and possibly from the caring of her child. Life changes in an extraordinary way for her.

The father is next. All that money and freedom he thought he was going to have by getting divorced? Sure, keep dreaming; the judge will likely fleece him for being so selfish and order his alimony payment and child support to be higher than normal given the circumstances. He will have no money to live on, no money to wine and dine anybody else. His social life won't be what he thought as the stigma of a father abandoning his disabled child will not sit well with any future mate, fair or not. He and his former wife have both lost financially. Guilt will set in about his child and depression will creep into his life as well.

The disabled child? Where do we start? He loses by far the most out of all three participants. The financial instability left in the father's absence is profound. Whatever child support or alimony payments are made to his mother will not come close to the replacement value of the income provided by his father. Daddy is no longer around to assist. The child loses the love from his mother as she is now doing all the chores in the family unit as she is the family unit. There's less time for caring, less time for reading, less time looking for services, which all adds up to a terrible situation for the child and for all the family members.

Unless your significant other is Lucifer, I implore all adults to think about the totality of what will happen if divorce occurs. Perhaps divorce from your spouse is okay; just know it's never okay to divorce your children. Each family is different and situations are not always static, but please think of the greater good and try your best to be unselfish.

Fairness is not that everybody gets the same; it's that everyone gets what they need.

There are so many events that will be missed, so many moments that will never occur because of the life you now lead. Dining out on Valentine's Day, vacations, stealing away for an afternoon's delight, meeting up with friends at a moment's notice are all compromised or never happen at all. *It is important to remember that this is no one's fault.*

Simply stated, stuff happens, so get over it already. This is the life you now have; go live it to the best of your ability. Do it for your spouse, do it for your other children, and most of all, do it for your disabled child.

Appreciate these types of moments: a beautiful sunrise/sunset, a handwritten note to/from your spouse, telling/hearing "I love you." Note that all of these acts of kindness have one thing in common: They cost nothing and give back everything.

Give yourself a break from the preconceived notion of what you should have been or what you could have done. That changed the moment you were given the opportunity to watch over a child with a disability. My dreams included being a CEO of a company, and I have been told by a few people that I should be doing that even now.

I wouldn't take that job today. My title is far superior at this juncture of my life. It's a badge I wear proudly; I am CEO of my family and dare I say I do a better job at this occupation than I ever would of overseeing a corporation. My heart is in this job title, my soul is alive because of this job, I have incomprehensible passion for this role.

I'll tell you why. Financially, most families with a disabled child live off of one paycheck while the other spouse is the primary caretaker, earning little to nothing. Neither one is better, neither holds an elevated status over the other, and neither one is more important. What is important is that the roles are *appreciated* by the spouses. My wife thanks me nearly every week for working so hard for us. I thank her along the same timeframe for doing what she does. In my eyes, hers is the more important role, simply because I could not do what she does. I do my job very well, but Laurie? Well let's just say she's an All-Star, a VIP, and a Superhero among mothers.

Ask anyone in my company, and they'll tell you that I am a valued employee, but who cares? Working hard is an attribute but in my opinion, it's one that may be given too much reverence in today's world. My wife is the most valuable resource in our family. She does not receive pay for her job; she doesn't know what a W2 or a 1099 form looks like. There is no monetary value associated with what she does.

That is why her job is so important; she does it gladly, without getting paid, and with that ever-present smile on her face. She gets her role and thanks me for allowing her to bring up our kids as a stay-at-home mom. It's like we are this throwback family, Ozzie and Harriett all over again. I work for us and she works for us; it's a beautiful dynamic that is often under-appreciated in today's world.

You don't have to be an economist to measure what each side brings to the family. That green presidential linen I bring home every week puts the roof over our heads, the car in our driveway, and the food in the fridge. My family needs me to earn, zero question about that. If I didn't earn as much, could we live somewhere else, drive a less-expensive car, and eat mac and cheese? You bet we could, and you can see the argument where money may not be as valuable as one thinks.

Contrast this with the amount of patience, love, and compassion a mother provides from a seemingly endless reservoir, and tell me, please, where can you buy these traits and how much would they cost to replace? I can't earn enough money to replace what Laurie does every day. There are simply not enough hours in the day. A mother's nurturing is the single most important thing in a child's life. The bride gets an A plus in this dimension.

I think a lot. I think when I'm driving, I think when I'm in school; I think all the time. My thoughts often bring me back to the early iteration of me. Specifically, about my days as a young father when my first-born, Ryan, arrived. I had been married before, and my first wife was a great mother also. I was a good father, but not great, and I often look back on what I could have done differently. When we divorced, it was exceptionally painful for me. I was angry, lost, and without my son. The worst day of my life up to that point was when the judge told me when I could not see my kid. Ryan was five when this happened, and his mother remarried and moved to Florida with him when he was twelve.

I'll never forget the day at the airport when he left for Florida; I cried like a baby. A boy needs his father at that age and poof, he was gone. And a father needs his boy just as much. I lost out on a lot of experiences with my son as did he with his dad. It is time we never get back.

Enter my son, Derek. Mr. Guy, as Ms. Laurie coined him when he was just a baby, has filled the void in time that I lost with Ryan. Derek will never be a man in the truest sense of the word, though. He will never drive, never vote, never get married. He, in essence, will never grow up.

And that is quite alright with me. I can relive those lost moments with Ryan through Derek. We take naps together, we watch football together, and we go for rides in the cwah, as he calls it, because that's what you do when you have young children, no matter how old they are.

I do not take this for granted, and I suck up every moment with Derek. He doesn't know who is playing football, doesn't know what a first down is, and it doesn't matter. What matters is that he is watching it with me. This is an example of appreciating the little things in life and always staying positive. *Caretakers are appreciative.*

If you go through life wanting what everyone else has, how can you ever work long enough to get the money to buy all those things? Try to imagine what that work week would look like. What is important in your life? If it's ruling the world, go for it; you go get that crown and all the trappings that go with it. Remember this saying if you choose this lifestyle, though: "Heavy is the head that wears the crown." If it's selling more of anything than any human ever sold in the history of humans, you go do that.

If it's a prophecy forced down your throat by a parent who is supposed to know what's good for you, take a breath and postulate what that really means...stop and think what is important in life. What is? Really think about it. Do you want your epitaph to say "Here lies Brian. That dude was the best damn salesman ever"? Do you want it to say, "Here lies Frankie. That guy worked so hard he never saw his family and he died before he could spend all the overtime money"? If you recall the dream I spoke of that Laurie and I had, it spoke of having that house, those trips, and some of the material things we have been conditioned to pursue. *Caretakers must embrace change.*

Derek changed all of that for us. And we love him for it. This way of thinking and prior conditioning is absolutely a game-changer. Where one day I would wake up and say how can I make more money to go on vacation or to put in the bank or for retirement, it now changes to how can I support this individual not only through the rest of our lives, but the rest of his as well? It changed our focus; it changed our compass to point towards what is real. What is real is love: love for someone else that you have a contract with, a contract to take care of, whatever the condition of that someone is.

Let's talk about the details of this contract. My previous belief about a contract included taking care of my wife forever and my children through their eighteenth birthday with the added bonus of helping with their college tuition. Included in this were the multiple borrowings from lending institutions to pay for cars, home equity loans, and the college tuition.

The primary goal was always to be debt-free when retirement comes knocking at your door. Then whatever bucket list items need to be checked off, you'd be ready willing and able to check them off. Hawaii, the ultimate old man's car, the Grand Marquis, an RV – all would be worthy pursuits. This was knowledge that was passed down generationally, an heirloom of finance if you will. There never was a word spoken about the possibility of a disability.

A disabled child changes so much: emotionally, the family dynamic, the stressors placed mentally on all, and possibly the most important, financially. Long after the emotions have been addressed (mostly through therapy), long after the other siblings have left the house, what we have left is the unanswerable question: What do we do with our disabled child when we are no longer on this planet?

Financially, we have to do the best job possible for our child. What that looks like for each family is as varied as the number of disabilities a child may encounter. Each family has its own issues, each has many siblings to contend with, and each battles for financial support from its parents, much like those baby sparrows that battle for the pieces of worm the parents work so hard to provide for them.

Think about the wholesale changes a disabled child brings about to the financial health and welfare of the entire family!

Speaking of therapy, I vividly remember a statement I made to my therapist thirty years ago: I want to provide for not only my family, but for generations to come. In other words, I wanted to lay the cornerstone, the framework for a successful business that could be run by future descendants. Was it a lofty goal? Yes it was, and one that was never realized, not necessarily because of Derek, but when the realization of his disability being one that is owned for a lifetime, the finance part had to change.

The truth lies somewhere in between my goal and Derek arriving on scene. I like to call it an evolution, a positive spin on life and how money isn't always king and honestly rarely is. Derek taught me that or better said, allowed my way of thinking to override what had always been taught to me. I learned that the little things in life can never be bought, no matter how wealthy one is.

The laughter at a stupid joke, the sunrise or sunset on a beautiful day, or the imperceptible knowledge that your disabled child has made a stride in life, no matter how miniscule. I've shopped at stores and even looked online, but I can't find any of these precious gifts for sale, for any amount of money.

Chapter 5

Derek's Arrival and How He Fits in Our Lives

"If you would be loved, love, and be lovable."

Benjamin Franklin

Daily seizures, a major operation on his skull at six months old, a diagnosis of autism, and developmental disability all had to be solved for – not only for Derek, but for my other two children, my wife, me, and the family unit. Taken one at a time, these are all major issues that could derail any one of us; taken together, my goodness, they could destroy our relationships with one another and be so detrimental to Derek.

I had been an extremely fortunate father, one who was present for each of his children's births. My firstborn, a son named Ryan, gave me the best day of my life. You only get to experience being a father for the first time once. From his birth, I was included in a special fraternity: fatherhood.

It was a measuring stick for a young man, a game-changer, a life event never to be repeated or forgotten. I was just outside my teenage years, at twenty-three years old, when I welcomed Ryan into my life. He was the best baby, cuteness defined, well-mannered, with dirty blond hair and a giggle that would make everyone else laugh. He was so ambitious, he couldn't wait the requisite nine months to be born and decided that he was marinated enough after eight months to join the rest of us humans.

My first wife and I were so lucky to have a child who was healthy, and we just accepted Ryan like that was the normal thing to do. It's hard to understand what others go through when you haven't experienced their joy or pain. We didn't know about any disability because we hadn't experienced it. It wasn't in our vernacular or our vocabulary. That would change, for me, one day….

I learned something very valuable in the moments immediately after Ryan's birth. The pediatrician announced a rather pedestrian sentence: ten fingers, ten toes. No kidding! Isn't that what all babies are supposed to have? It is something we simply take for granted: After pregnancy, after the birthing is complete, our child will be normal. _Until the day comes when he or she is not normal._

It is then that we come to grips with the reality that thousands of children are born each day who are not normal, who suffer from some type of disability. It is then that we realize how lucky, how fortunate we are to have had a healthy child. It's why the joy is so complete for a father and especially for a mother, who gets to hear the heartbeat and the gentle kicking of her soon-to-be-born child. The elation and absolute nirvana one experiences at becoming parents can quickly be tempered by the acknowledgment that one's child has been born with a disability.

Subliminally, another crossroads is at hand and the choices of "why?" or "woe is me" can be replaced by "how can I help and what do I need to do to make my child's life the best it can possibly be?" There are a number of paths one can take when presented with the news of a less-than-healthy child: disbelief, why me, acceptance, advocate, isolation, etc. I'm certain once again that most folks go through nearly every one of these soon after the news is given. It's natural; it's human to experience these feelings.

Accept that you aren't Superman or some cold-blooded soul who can't understand what just happened. The goal here is to allow yourself and your partner to feel the emotions as time passes. It's an absolute given that you will think about each of these, and there is nothing amiss with your psyche to feel these one at a time, all together, or some combination thereof. It's a lot to handle; give yourself the time to work them out in your own way, and be respectful of your partner's path as well. There is no correct way, no tried-and-true measure that works for all. Give yourself a break, or two or three if you need them.

Do not underestimate the impact of joining a specific support group. If you can't find a local chapter with your child's disability, look for a support group that has something similar. It's not the particular disability that is of real importance for the support group; it's the inclusion and knowledge you will receive that is important. Here's why: validation. How does a person recognize normality? It's a not-so-complex question that gets exceptionally difficult when faced with rearing a disabled child.

Here's the definition of normal: "conforming to a standard, usual, typical, or expected." There is nothing normal about caring for a disabled child. Whose standard will you be using, what exactly is typical for a disabled child, and usual? I'm not sure what that looks like either. The support group you just joined will help you with all of these feelings.

There will be validation that frees your mind from some sorrow, from some hopelessness, and lets you focus on the important aspects of bringing up your child. Your normal might start to take shape there. If not there, some other construct will help with this. It could be that you know someone, perhaps a good friend, a close relative, a therapist, or even your own research, that will help you to understand what it means to be in a normal state of mind regarding you and your disabled child's relationship.

It is exceptionally important that you fully embrace this new normal. Measuring sticks for your child will now be altered in a way that is different, not bad. Learn the difference between the two. Where a regular child may throw a football thirty yards after just a few minutes of being taught how to throw it, your child may not even want anything to do with a football.

Measure them by effort, determination, and fairness. Do not measure them by something that cannot be attained given their restraints. Keep their dreams and your dreams alive, but be realistic in your thoughts. This quote is attributed by some to Einstein: "Everyone is a genius, but if you measure a fish by its ability to climb a tree, it will live its whole life believing it is stupid." Set a goal for your child that is achievable. If they aren't hitting their goals, take time to readjust and set attainable goals.

Let feedback be your best friend, and don't be too hard on either your child or yourself. That doesn't do anyone any good at all. The best place to be is with your child, encouraging and advocating. *As a caretaker, this is your new normal.*

The parent's expectation of a normal child is so great because it's rare that a child will be disabled. However, that has changed recently. There are dozens of reasons that are debatable; I am not here to debate them. I am only here to state that the rate of disabled children has gone up remarkably in the last twenty years in one specific area: autism. When Derek was born in 1994, the rate was about one in five hundred. Today that rate stands at around one in fifty-nine.

AUTISM PREVALENCE, 1975-2009

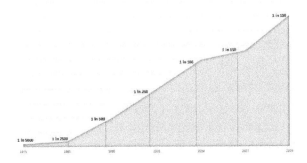

For our purposes, the reasons don't really matter. The root causes still lead us to a path of a disabled child who must be cared for by a family. Again, take this as a positive; there is now much information and many support groups that offer help, aid, and assistance precisely because of how common autism has become. You see, when a problem becomes common, more resources are levied against it so that a cure can be eventually found. With autism in particular, it is crucial to gain early intervention, as the quicker one becomes immersed in a program, the higher the likelihood of their quality of life being better.

The next child in succession was a female. I had told anyone within earshot that she was going to be a boy. I do mean everybody; ask anyone I know! I was so confident I was having another boy, I just knew it. I was never more wrong in my life. This baby pops out and she has no man parts; trust me, I'm looking for the one thing that will let me know I have another boy. There is no periscope.

I ask myself, what was I going to do with this girl, this female, of all things? Turns out, everything! We danced, we played baseball, we wrestled, and most important, she taught me to be a better dad. She took the edge off of me, knocking my testosterone back down a few notches.

It was on her born day that I started to be a more complete person, a more complete man, a more complete human. My daughter is named Haley Lyn, and she has never disappointed me. She was, however, in the running for the title of the world's worst baby. I mean it. Haley would cry all the time, like 24/7 all the time. The doctors said it was colic, but I think she already knew I was her dad, and that this was the cause of her incessant wailing.

My wife was wonderfully patient with her, taking her for rides in the car or walking and rocking her at all hours of the day and night. I'm so proud of her for those moments in her life. She easily could have done things differently but didn't. She *always* did the right thing when it came to parenting.

She was born to do this most important job of all the vocations in the entire world. She worked hard at it and never gave up, always encouraging Haley as a baby, and it continued on into her adult years. Ms. Haley is now twenty-six, and we couldn't be prouder of what she has accomplished thus far in her short life. I'm a proud father who tells you that his daughter has a Master's Degree in Psychology, having graduated with a 4.0 GPA. She is an even better person than a student, and that tells you everything about my daughter that you need to know. This was yet another lesson my wife and I learned that would help us with Derek. Patience is the ultimate trait a parent must possess when a disabled child is part of the family.

You've now seen a brief snapshot into my married life with two of my children, one from each of my two marriages. It's probably pretty run of the mill, normal, and within eighty percent of what other families go through every day around the world.

So how does my son Derek fit into this family dynamic? The short answer is he doesn't fit as well or as easily as my two others do. What it doesn't mean is we won't do everything in our power to see that he does fit as best he can while being fair to the rest of the family.

In this environment, the devil is in the details. There has always got to be a family solution and a backup plan and flexibility built in or on the fly. The best-laid plans can be destroyed in the blink of an eye. It doesn't mean the family still can't have a good time; they just have to be flexible too. This trait should at all costs be modeled by the two parents and taught by example to the children impacted by the disabled child.

It really is a teachable moment in life where optimism will always win the day and flexibility has to be built in to nearly every decision one makes in life. It's our job as parents and teachers to ensure this gets passed down to our children. Keep the family on the same page, and life will be much easier for all participants.

At three months old, Derek was progressing normally outside of these episodes of intermittently staring blankly into space. We'd get his attention eventually, and he would respond appropriately ... until one day he didn't and stared blankly again. But this time it was accompanied by a body long stiffness, the kind you see when someone gets knocked out. His lips were blue. It was time for an ambulance.

After many consultations and visits and doctors' offices, we were told he was indeed suffering from seizures, and we would need to start a medication protocol. During this time, my first son Ryan was living with his mother, and Haley was not yet two years old, so they were shielded from any of the trauma one would expect a child to experience when seeing a sibling suffer seizures. Hell, I was scared, and I was the adult. It is important as caretakers to be available for your other children when they experience a sibling acting so abnormally.

Derek's operation at six months old was a bit more intrusive for all. My son Ryan was eleven at the time, and I had the conversation with him about Derek's operation. He was a pretty level-headed kid, asked a few questions that I answered, and probably went out to play with his G.I. Joes after we spoke.

Haley was about to turn two and no conversation happened with her, but she did spend a week with her Memere as we would be in NYC for that period of time. I will be forever grateful to that woman for watching our daughter. The next six months were critical for Derek not bumping his head so that he could heal properly, and believe or not, even with a two-year-old,
we managed to escape with Derek's skull intact! A lot of effort went into making that safety net happen, and my wife did an unbelievable job balancing Derek and Haley during that time. She really is a wonderful mother.

When I noticed Derek not progressing through the normal childhood benchmarks, I spoke with Laurie who initially dismissed it as most mothers are wont to do. We gave it a month, but it became apparent something was amiss. The classic signs of being dissociative, limited-to-no eye contact and a general withdrawal all signaled a likely autism diagnosis.

Our pediatrician and neurologist confirmed our fears, and we were about to experience yet another pitfall we knew nothing about. This issue was the hardest of all to communicate to everyone. Seizures and the operation were solvable; Derek was taking medication that nearly cured all his seizures, and the operation had healed his skull cleanly so they were both mostly in our rearview mirror. But autism is a condition that could last for decades and severely impact the quality of life for everyone in the family.

Let's talk a bit more about inclusion and what it means for all children and families. We lived in back of a golf course, within a couple of houses of a bike path and about a quarter mile away from a sports complex that includes ballfields, playgrounds, basketball courts, and a skate park – all activities any child could enjoy.

It would be an absolute travesty if we didn't include Derek in our plans for any of the above fun events. Will he go out and pitch a no-hitter or perform a 720 front-side stalefish, or dunk a basketball? Of course he won't. Can we enable him to watch a baseball game with us by walking to the complex instead of driving, giving him the ability to see nature and interact with other folks along the way? Sure!

Can we place him alongside the basketball courts and allow him to throw the ball in from time to time or to actually score a basket? He can do this, and it warms my heart. The playground is probably best for him, so that's where we can spend time for him, with him, and watch him have a little fun. Listen, there are days when he doesn't want to do anything and nothing will bring him joy at any event; so what, bring him anyway just for inclusion purposes. He's part of the family, and is it any different than bringing a daughter to a hockey game she may want no part of? She won't be happy either, and that's part of life. It really is about creating memories. One day we'll all be sitting back in our rocking chairs and reminiscing about the good ol' days. Your job is to make sure you have enough to remember, including your disabled child/adult. *Caretakers make the best of every situation and stay positive and flexible.*

I'm going to give you proof positive of two events in our lives that sit at the top of my mind. One is in the late summer, early fall 2016, at a place called The Big E in Springfield, Mass. Laurie, Derek, and I walked up to the entrance to purchase tickets and before we could get in, a man approached us and offered to give us two discounted tickets as he couldn't use them.

There were other people in line before us, and I'm assuming, probably correctly, that he had empathy for our son who we were pushing in a handicapped stroller. We saved twenty dollars that day but that's not the lesson; we were recognized and were the benefactors of a wonderful human being who could have given those tickets to anyone but chose to make a handicapped child's day.

During the day, as this is a farm-based exposition, we would see animals in pens with crowds all around them. In almost every case, people would turn around and offer Derek an unobstructed view. Allow me to opine here; the demographic at The Big E is one of working folk and in my tenure on this planet, I've found the closer you are to the working man, the more empathy you possess.

The second instance is the Luray Caverns in Luray, Va. It's a beautiful place of underground wonderment that all ages can enjoy. The reason I picked this spot to visit on one of our trips was that it is handicapped accessible. For an old guy, I'm in pretty good shape, and I stay that way precisely because of Derek. As you might imagine, there was a major change in elevation once inside the caverns. I did okay by myself pushing Derek around in his carriage until the last rise, which was slippery and steep. I made it work. Here's the best part: I had folks lining up to help push him the rest of the way up. I did not ask; every single one of them volunteered to assist. I am grateful that they did and so is Derek.

The moral of the story is don't be limited by what you think you or your child can visit. You'll miss out on a whole world of experiences, and life is way too short for that. The general public will help; society has recognized our less fortunate at a level not seen before in history. Businesses are completely aware of including people with disabilities. It's good for business to include all folks.

I don't recall the exact amount we spent at Luray Caverns, but if they weren't accommodating they wouldn't get any of my money. Do what you think you can't accomplish and when you accomplish it, smile, and go get you some more of that....

Chapter 6

The Operation

Give me six hours to chop down a tree and I will spend the first four sharpening the axe."

Abraham Lincoln

"I know a guy," is an overused soliloquy in my home state of Rhode Island. It simply means that one of your friends knows someone who can get a job done or get something for you; sometimes those things are bought with cash, with no receipt. This time it meant something far more serious, life changing for us in its scope, with devastating consequences potentially. The "guy" in this case was Dr. Carlos Canton, a pediatric neurologist who would take us to a place no parent wants to go: major surgery for their child.

In this example, there was no other option; this was not elective surgery. This operation was lifesaving in that Derek would ultimately perish had this not been performed. If I remember correctly, Dr. Canton was about the eighth doctor we had consulted about Derek and his condition, and he knew immediately where to steer us.

At six months old, our son was going to have corrective surgery that required taking the top half of his skull off, breaking it into suitable, usable pieces, and rebuilding it to resemble a normal skull. The condition Derek had was called craniosynostosis. Dr. Goodrich, thanks to Dr. Canton, was the doctor who gave us this news in Montefiore Hospital in the Bronx, New York City.

I remember it well. It was a cold, dreary weekday in May of 1995, and our world got a tad more focused that day. It brought my wife and me together in a way ordinary, run-of-the-mill love just couldn't do. We were now fighting for something so much more important than our love for each other. We were fighting for our son, someone we had made together, someone we were responsible for. Derek's love would make us stronger, not weaker, and it was this driving force that allowed us to become a cohesive unit, a team that would weather that storm and many others to follow.

The news was shocking; I didn't even know what craniosyno-stosis was and couldn't spell it if you spotted me the first ten letters. The news may be akin to what those who go in for a physical get: some type of unsuspecting news, maybe a diagnosis of cancer or some other lifechanging news that is hard to accept, hard to wrap logic around.

My wife and I were sitting in the doctor's office, a small room filled with shrunken heads, talking to a man who just told us what the diagnosis of our son was and what we had to do to get it fixed. Normally, I am never at a loss for words, ever. My wife looked at me, I looked at her, and we shared a blank, unknowing, frightened stare. It was like Dr. Goodrich had asked us to perform calculus, in a foreign language, under water, blindfolded. "What did he just say, what does this all mean, what the heck do we do now?"

We were truly stunned and probably felt exactly like that deer in the headlights everyone talks about. The good doctor asked us if we had any questions and we just looked at him, stam-mered a bit, and said, uh, no...he then reminded us that we should be asking about the recovery time, how long the surgery would last, and the level of danger Derek would be exposed to. You know all those things that responsible parents ask, except at that moment, we were not responsible; we were simply overwhelmed by this relatively easy piece of news. We were not capable, because we were not prepared to hear what we heard. *We were inexperienced.*

Allow me to explain in layman's terms what this particular diagnosis of craniosynostosis is and what it means in the arena of disability. Craniosynostosis is when the skull becomes malformed because of many different causes. In Derek's case, the best explanation is that his sutures in his skull and at least one of the two soft spots prematurely closed in his still forming skull while in utero.

Derek's body, not realizing what was happening, continued to send calcium to the skull with devastating results. His head grew in size to that of nearly a full-size adult, and coupled with the fact that I had a naturally large head, spelled doom for a natural childbirth. Mothers' pathways of birth don't allow for such an increase in skull size.

This is exactly how some mothers died in childbirth before the advent of Caesarean section birthing. There was simply no way for the child to pass, and the resulting trauma to the baby and the excessive bleeding by the mother often led to death for one or both. I'm glad we live in this century.

I cannot imagine the severity of sorrow and loss that the surviving children and spouse must have felt when this occurred. Did I mention that this surgery would have to happen as quickly as possible as the skull does not stay malleable forever? Once it sets, in most cases at about six months, surgery would not be an option. Our little guy, our pride and joy, would go in for surgery on his half-year anniversary of life.

His surgery would require an ear-to-ear incision, and the top half of his skull would be removed. Dr. Goodrich was an expert in this area and had done many of these same surgeries before. The skull, while excised from the head, would be examined and eventually broken up into suitable pieces for rebuilding. In the good doctor's words, "they found a suitable piece in the back of the skull and made his forehead out of it." Almost exactly how I used to break up a cases of juice and mix them up and put them back together, just a little bit more complicated.

Medical professionals have a bonding agent they call bone glue, and they proceeded to break apart the rest of his skull and patiently piece back together what would be Derek's new skull cap. It's like when you bring your convertible down to the restorer and he sends you back home with a shiny new vinyl top, only a tad more difficult!

Once this part of the operation was completed, the new piece was gently put back into place, and they bonded, sutured, and sewed Derek's skull up, folding the skin back onto the scalp, and suturing that for a finished job.

The surgery took about nine hours, and time stood still like it never had before. Thoughts raced through our minds that never did before. Will Derek be okay, what happens if he isn't, what if he…? It's a time where honesty and reality intersect with an acute fragility that only parents know when their child is having a lifesaving operation. But still, we had each other.

Suddenly the waiting room door opened and there stood Dr. Goodrich, our man of the hour, his protective mask hanging by his throat, his white beard providing a fatherly, comforting feeling, his soft disposition relaying the news we both wanted to hear: Derek came through the surgery just fine and all went well. He explained to us the next two days Derek would be in pediatric ICU and if all went well we should be able to go home in a week. Our emotional demons faded away; despondency was replaced with relief that our son would be okay. The confidence the good doctor had in his voice told us so.

He departed the waiting room, and my wife and I were left alone to digest what just occurred. We hugged each other, cried a little, and took a couple of deep breaths because at least this part of the journey was complete. The waiting room was a corollary for what we had just gone through: fearful and dumbfounded, alone, and with emptiness in our souls we had felt upon arrival.

When we exited, we were stronger, more knowledgeable, and more confident about our and our son's future. Our emotions had been taken for a ride, but the apex of these emotions had been reached. We had survived this like our son had survived his operation. Another step taken, another step conquered. And we stayed positive.

The next seven days were a test of our resolve for Derek and for each other. Our initial visit to see him was both frightening and bittersweet; we had been told to expect some swelling and disfigurement. What we saw was exactly that; Derek could have been cast in a Rocky movie as the baby Stallone character. He was swollen alright, eyes completely shut, and the areas around his eyes were bruised and discolored.

He was hooked up to more machines than I'd ever seen before, with tubes and wires running everywhere. He was bandaged from his eyebrows on up in what seemed like five pounds of white gauze. It was hard to look at.

His hands were tied to his bed rails to prevent him from doing any damage to himself. My wife and I were in a stupor emotionally; how do you prepare for a moment like this? She did what moms do; she soothed her son and touched him lovingly. We would spend one more day with Derek in ICU, and the next five days would be one of remarkable recovery. Infants recover incredibly quickly, and on the seventh day we were allowed to leave the hospital and take our journey home.

To think that a baby who just had the top half of his skull removed, broken apart, glued, and screwed back together, and had extensive plastic surgery and had it put back in place would be allowed to go home in a week stretches the bounds of believability. Just over six months ago, we were awaiting a baby who would be like any other baby: healthy, normal, vibrant, and energetic. Ten fingers, ten toes.

I remember leaving Montefiore Hospital with our bionic baby boy and realizing we now had a special package to take care of. Our son was now new and improved, and we should see to it that he received the best possible care from us. This thought is as fresh in my mind as it was then, some twenty-five years ago. Together we would stand, resolute in our dedication to our son.

We drove him home from NYC, which is never fun, and although I've delivered millions of dollars in product throughout my career as a truck driver, never did I have more precious cargo with me in the backseat of my car. I drove cautiously on the way home, relieved that Derek would be okay and apprehensive about the days and weeks ahead of us.

Here we were, pulling into the driveway of our home, and this would normally be a time for celebration but we had to "Derek proof" the house. Our daughter Haley was about to turn two, and her brother just had major skull surgery. We set up our house with blankets and towels to have no corners, no sharp edges that Derek could potentially hit his head on. *Caretakers adjust and improvise* on the fly.

He pretty much lived in his baby walker for the next six months for his protection, and it worked out wonderfully. He never had an instance where he whacked his head on anything and for that we are thankful and grateful.

Years later, about two decades or so, the irony of sitting in a doctor's office full of shrunken heads hit me like a ton of bricks. Derek would have yet another operation, by the same doctor, at the same hospital, so really, what else would you expect a doctor who operates on skulls to have in his office?

Derek's second operation on his skull, this time at the base, was much less intrusive, and the two options we had discussed beforehand would only be apparent after Dr. Goodrich started the surgery. Thankfully, the easier route was the best option, and his recovery was uneventful. When I think about those visits with my wife at the doctor's office, I often think of those skulls on display. I suppose they are the lexicon of his business, the very language he speaks to when performing his surgeries.

I've been in the beverage business for decades, and my office is littered with different types of empty bottles I've sold through-out the years. I could have used a bottle or two of whiskey after all I had gone through. Still, the mysteries of the mind are elusive, and the skulls are a great reminder that there is so much left to learn about in this universe of ours. The caretaker in us gets to explore this universe.

This operation would leave multiple scars on Derek, on my wife, on me, and the rest of the family. The easy scars to see were visible on Derek's scalp. The not so easy were on the inside of his skull and somewhere in his mind. I would wonder how much pain he felt, physically and emotionally. In an odd way, perhaps his lack of comprehension would alleviate most mental turmoil and anguish he may have felt. I can only hope this was the case.

I think parents want to naturally fix their child with a Band-Aid or the wipe away of a tear. It's easy to understand that where there is blood, place a Band-Aid; when a tear forms, provide a tissue. It's hard when there is little emotion, an exceptionally high pain tolerance, and with a child who doesn't feel emotions normally. How do you effectively heal a child who is non-communicative and cannot verbalize when he's in need of pain medication? We really had to dial in to his non-verbal cues to assess his situation.

When adversity hits, you learn pretty quickly that you can depend on a very small circle of people to assist with your needs. They include you, your spouse, your immediate family members, and if you're really lucky, a close friend or two.

Everyone outside of your spouse can help with the incidental trips to the store, the homemade pie or cake brought over, but the intimacy of those deepest emotions can only truly be shared by the parents, with each other, alone. The seriousness of having a disabled child can be tiring, and a strong front must be put on most of the time. Remember to take the time to be vulnerable with your partner. It does not show weakness; just the opposite, it shows strength. Strength in the fact that you recognized you needed help, and when the conversation is over and the tears have dried, you can find comfort with each other.

It's simple math; two are stronger than one and two caretakers care better than one.

For a man, this is traditionally and exponentially harder than for a woman. We've been trained from a young age to be tough, we must have the "S" on our chests, we must protect at all costs. I am really guilty of this but getting better at it. I get stuck in the "my wife and family need me" mentality, and I do a good job at self-monitoring. However, I know deep down inside that I am of no use to my family if I am unstable myself. You've heard the saying about wolves; the strength is in the pack. *Be the wolf pack of caretakers for your pup.*

We have a saying at the house called "get things done." What did you do at work today, honey? I got things done. It's a microcosm of life. When situations get heated or there seems to be an insurmountable task at hand, break it down into small manageable parts. The unassailable mountaintop now appears to be vulnerable to summiting.

Ask anyone who has climbed Everest; they don't just walk up to the Himalayas and say I think I'll climb this bad boy today. I urge you to Google the process and see how difficult this project is. None of it is intellectually difficult. All the steps it takes to summit the mountain are just that: a means to an end. Once you complete these small parts, it'll give you incentive and drive to finish the job, or get things done. You can see the completion bar in your mind filling up towards the end goal. When you feel you are starting to get overwhelmed, remember to break it down and start at step one. Finish that step and move on, and repeat as necessary to reach the end zone.

This inexperience I spoke of would never happen again. We would always prepare for our next dilemma, our next hurdle to cross, or our next obstacle to overcome. My wife is the queen of research, and I think she was an early writer of code for Google. This is what special needs parents do: They research; boy, do they research. They ask questions, they join support groups, and they get prepared. We have to learn to blaze our own trails, light the darkness, and rely on no one but ourselves. Where there is no path, we make one. We have to stay motivated for ourselves, for our children, for our lives.

We have to be that salesperson who gets told "no" fifteen times, but has the resolve and tenacity to close the sixteenth sale at the end of a long day. He can take solace in the fact that he performed at his best at the time he wanted desperately to give up. He takes that winning attitude with him the next day and knows, deep within himself, that should he encounter fifteen prospective buyers and they all say no, number sixteen is waiting for him, just ripe for the closing.

He knows, because he's done it in the past and can relate to that success currently and into the future. He's built this confidence one brick at a time and has failed many more times than he succeeded, yet he knows he can do it. It's this type of emotional conditioning we must build, both within ourselves and our families.

Please keep in mind that this is never easy, never predestined, never been done before, this life of ours. It is *our* life, no one else's! Change is such a significant part of everyone's life, but the difference between what most people experience and what parents of disabled children experience is two-fold: the frequency of changes, and the severity of changes. Where a regular family might decide on a change of venue for a restaurant on a family night out, we as parents of disabled kids know not to make plans at all and cherish the moments we can get out with our families.

Regular families pick and choose an activity like basketball or cheerleading for their children at school. We might bring our kids to their events and secretly wish our children could be playing second base or be waving the pom-poms to the beat of the band. Where there are options available to regular families, we manufacture our own options; we fight for what is right for our children. Caretakers prepare for life. *We play the hand that's been dealt to us.*

Chapter 7

The Autism Diagnosis

Hope is the thing with feathers that perches in the soul and sings the tunes without the words and never stops at all.

Emily Dickinson

Being present at all of my kids' births was an experience I would never trade for all of the money in the world. To see, with your own eyes, the process of birth that leads into life is incomparable in this universe. It's a feeling of pride, of unspoken grandeur, something to be ecstatic about, something to be savored, and something exceptional.

It's nine months of gestation and two people to provide the genetic material needed for one human. And it's your human to love and hold and shape and form. It is an awesome event that takes one's breath away. Take a moment and equate this event with anything else you've ever been a party to. Go ahead. I'm waiting….

This feeling of accomplishment only grows over time. All the little milestones they approach and conquer, mostly with your help and guidance, and eventually on their own, provide the closure on the feedback loop of parenting done the right way. It's a feeling I'm still high on after all these years.

My oldest is now thirty-six , and although he hasn't hit any new milestones lately, I'm still in awe of who he has grown into as an adult. Same for my baby girl, now twenty-six and following in her older brother's footsteps of succeeding at most things she tries. And yes, I'm proud of Derek, our disabled child. The little man has had a tougher road than most can fathom, but he's still here, still fighting, still living, and still smiling.

His autism is not as severe as when it was officially diagnosed, and for that we are thankful. We're staying positive and looking for the silver lining every chance we get. It's what we do and what we've become, just ordinary people looking for the best possible life for our family.

I did not know it at the time, but Ryan's and Haley's births were a measuring stick for me. I thought I knew what to expect the third time around. However, I was not prepared to see what Derek looked like when he arrived in November 1994. There is something you need to know; my wife is tough as nails, and you never hear her complain. I may have seen her cry emotionally but never from physical pain, until that day, the day she gave birth to our son.

When she was in labor with Derek and we were at the hospital, she started to experience severe pain. Remember, this was her second child and Derek should have come along a bit easier. My wife asked for the doctor, and I knew something was wrong. Derek was taken by C-section and the reason was all too apparent; his head was very large and extremely misshapen. The pediatrician didn't have to say a word. My heart sank as I knew this was far from normal. Our journey had begun.

We named our son Derek Connor, and we accepted him into our lives like any family would. He was a present waiting to be opened, pages of a book not yet written, a teacher of love to his parents. I wanted to name him D'Eric, to honor Laurie's father, a man he would never meet, but we ultimately settled on the traditional spelling. Eric, Laurie's dad, would have eaten this kid up; his grandchild would have been first on his list of priorities.

At fifty-eight, my age now, he would have been in the sweet spot of his life, a pension waiting for him for his service at the water company, a house that had long been paid off, and no material wants.

Derek, I'm afraid, would have been spoiled rotten, and Laurie and I would have been okay with that outcome. We often speak openly about how unfortunate it is that the two people who would have been so happy with Derek present in their lives are no longer with us. My mother Ellie would have been that second person. To say that my mother would have showered Derek with love is like saying the sun might shine on the Sahara today. It would have been a daily ritual, something I miss for my son. Meme, as she would have been called, would have been the loving glance, the comforting touch, and the voice of reason should Derek, Laurie, or I need it.

We now provide all these articles of love to Derek and just as important, to each other. We choose to deliver the message that our silenced loved ones cannot. We speak for the departed and the mute. We do not choose to be pessimistic or to say "why us?" We take the high road and teach what we've been taught so well: to stay unselfish and let love lead the way. Your strength as a person, as parents, as caretakers is in your love and your love comes from your bloodlines.

Sadly, a cruel situation happens with autistic children. They develop just about normally from twelve months or so to one and a half years, and then the change starts to happen. They grow distant, almost imperceptibly at first; they avoid eye contact; and they start to grow cold emotionally. They can get belligerent, short-tempered, and not listen to directions. Certain foods are all they will consume; this week it might be Twinkies for breakfast, lunch, and dinner; next week, next month, it might be graham crackers. If it's a red marker they want to write with, you better have about eight dozen on hand, because no other color marker will do.

Their behaviors can turn physically violent in the most extreme cases, and the condition is often accompanied by seizures and tics. It is heartbreaking to witness these events as they unfold. This is your child and what is happening here? Why is this happening? We did everything right, listened to the doctor's advice, took the prenatal vitamins, exercised, and still this happens?

The parents are certain that they have done something wrong, that they must not have given enough love, or have been too cold themselves. Nothing is further from the truth. Take the guilt and the blame and throw them away in some dark abyss where they belong, never to be heard from again. The true causes are not yet known, but scientists are working diligently to uncover information and research points to a genetic component in at least some of the cases.

Hidden guilt is an insidious creature. It will live in you for as long as you allow it to, no more, no less. It must be identified and be released from your mindset. Nothing a parent has done could have caused autism in their child. Having a drug problem, having a cold partner emotionally, or eating the wrong diet do not make a child autistic. The sooner a parent can come to grips with this, the better for them and their child.

There are so many things that must be done, and guilt cannot be in the way if they are to be done effectively. Free yourself and your child from this energy-sapping emotion. It will do no good to anyone to manifest guilt into your daily ritual. The important thing to remember is this is what you have right here, right now, and you must find a way to manage it effectively.

Practice doing your best work on being in the present moment. Yesterday has come and gone, and will never be lived again except in your memories. Tomorrow has not yet come and worry will rob you of the satisfaction of today. Your disabled child or adult needs you right now, not yesterday and certainly not tomorrow, because you don't know what's to come.

The problems we face as caretakers require us to be here right now, ready for action, sometimes ready for superhuman actions. It's best to live in that space. Your child deserves that of you, and you deserve that of you. One of my coworkers would remind me that all we have is the present time, that nothing else really matters, and I believe he was spot on in his assessment.

Here's a thumbnail sketch of Derek at eighteen months: mostly muted, no emotion, unfeeling, and eating Pringles Sour Cream and Onion potato chips from a can. The cries you hear do not emanate from Derek; they are the cries and the tears falling slowly to the wooden floor beneath the feet of his parents.

Unfortunately, my son started life with the deck stacked against him. This was not the first major health issue he had faced. Dr. Goodrich changed Derek's life and our lives forever, performing this operation that allowed Derek a chance at a better life.

I will forever be grateful to that man for his skills and his compassion. I could never pay him commensurate to how our lives have been enriched by his actions. He wouldn't take the money anyway; it's just his nature. Tell me where do you find people like this? You find them when you carry the privilege of a disabled child with you, that's where.

Fittingly, it is at this juncture of your life that you realize there is more good than evil, more for you to learn than not, and that your best self is not even close to who you are currently. This is a gift of life and a lesson that you never would have experienced had you not had a disabled child; this is why our journey is special. Why do you think they call disabled children, "special needs"?

This is why you stay positive, never, ever, give up, and be truly thankful for what you have rather than what you don't have. There are so many folks on this planet who would willingly trade places with you. It's why I almost never complain. I am faithfully aware of how lucky I am at this stage of my life.

A sobering statistic to understand is that eighty percent of parents with autistic children get divorced; Laurie and I were going to be "the twenty percenters," those people who defied the odds, with help from Derek and his love. We would choose to be optimistic, no matter what. We would look for the good in the situation, no matter what. We would learn to be both flexible and supportive. We had each other, we had Derek's love, and that would be our glue, our cement, our cohesive bond that would bind us together for the short haul, for the long haul. We were in this trip of a lifetime together like our wedding song.

Derek was also diagnosed with epilepsy and his seizures were sometimes severe, sometimes mild, but always frightening. When he was less than two, he started having seizures that scared us to the point of having a phone in our hands ready to dial 911 if he didn't stop in a few seconds. These seizures were typically along these lines: he'd stop breathing, and he would become nearly catatonic and so stiff physically that you could pick him up with one hand. Maybe my memory isn't completely accurate, but I thought I saw him start to turn blue on a few occasions. He was diagnosed with being developmentally delayed, another obstacle for him and our family to overcome.

My wife decided to make a picture book for Derek, made from Velcro pieces laminated in plastic that he could easily decipher. Just another example of creatively putting in place what was missing to allow Derek to become the best version of Derek he could be. It was painstakingly slow for Derek to grasp the concept, but he did, after a lot of encouragement. Once a baseline was established, he would go on to have a vocabulary of about fifty words, no small feat for him to master.

Considering the average person uses about five hundred different words a day, this was a huge win for all of us, another small example of never giving up, of staying focused and persevering. There isn't anything that most parents won't do for their children, but disabled kids take that concept to a whole other level. You find that extra fire in your soul, that extra push that sends you over the top for your kids. They deserve it, and you get a benefit as well. You get the chance to be a better human, and everyone around you in your circle of family and friends benefits as well.

Most children will learn a new skill and build off that skill until they master it. Usually the building will only stop because of lack of interest, and it's on to the next skill. Please understand as caretakers you have a baseline that will not move as quickly as other children's baselines do. *And that is completely okay.*

Work with them on a simple task, and give them the time and patience to accomplish that task at their own pace.

Different disabilities will require different levels of time, patience, and love to see a skill learned...and sometimes that skill doesn't come. That's okay too; there are other skills out there just waiting to be accomplished by your child. Help them in whatever way you can.

Chapter 8

When Two Roles Coexist; Individual and Spouse

"Keep love in your heart. A life without it is like a sunless garden when the flowers are dead."

Oscar Wilde

Like a penguin that stands guard over its hatchling, one parent must always be available for assistance with a disabled child. They must brave the weather, and all predation that comes their way. That availability can come in many forms: help with feeding, with bathroom hygiene duties, showering, help with seizures that need attention, and help in the form of empathy. The child becomes the center of your universe, the reason you exist. He must take center stage because of the extraordinary care that must be provided for him by a caretaker. That caretaker is a parent or both parents, or if you're really fortunate, a sibling or trusted friend.

When groceries run low, when prescriptions need filling, when the snow needs to be shoveled, it is by one parent, one guardian. The other watches, assists, and holds a hand, dries a tear, blows a nose, or wipes a butt. The dividing line is pretty clear; the disabled child comes first.

When you're in your twenties or early thirties as most new parents are, you want to have fun with your partner. You bonded with each other initially; in most cases, children came later. Most parents do have a plan in place where they will enjoy each other for a predetermined time and plan for a child when they are ready.

The relationship between a husband and wife can deteriorate quickly, though, when a special needs child is introduced. That one-on-one time that a couple takes for granted in a normal marriage can sometimes get lost in a hurry when this occurs. Most couples have the luxury of choosing Saturday or Friday nights to go out to see the local show or dine at a restaurant.

Not so with the family dynamic that includes a disabled person. Sadly, this fracturing of the husband-wife pairing is at the root of the high divorce rate families experience when a disabled child is included in the reporting. It's so easy for me to see why. "Honey, I'm going bowling with the fellas. I'll be home around midnight." Or "Sweetie, I'll be out dancing with the girls; don't wait up." Like there would be any chance of any waiting up by either party. With a chance to catch up on some sleep, the other party is slumbering away.

Sometimes separate memories are created out of necessity as one parent either needs some time out alone or with his or her friends. It's like you're living two lives; one with your friends but not your spouse, and the other with your spouse. Both are okay; just remember where your bread is buttered and be sure to include your spouse when the luxury of a night out is presented. These nights out are truly a gift; use the time to reconnect with the person you married.

If you choose to embrace this lifestyle, the rewards can be life-altering. A funny thing happens along the journey; you learn to really appreciate the little things in life. Why? Because your life demands it. You owe it to yourself, you owe it to your spouse, and you owe it to your child. The kiss in the morning and the one at night when you come home to your loved one, the coffee made just the way you like it, your favorite flavor of Ben

& Jerry's in the freezer, or a favorite meal prepared all speak to a higher level of unselfishness.

It's a trait that one must have intrinsically, although it must often be embellished along the way. Without this, life is made much more difficult; there is animosity in the air. *Caretakers care for each other too.*

New cars wear out, fancy clothes go out of style, and money depreciates. For the price of a nice new jewelry piece, you could easily afford about fifty bouquets of flowers. Instead of that tenth bottle of expensive perfume, why not bring your wife her favorite takeout meal or surprise her with a meal you made yourself? Trust me; your hubby-prepared meal doesn't have to taste as good as hers. The time spent together will take care of any deficiencies in the kitchen.

Convincingly, it can be found in the Joneses' vacation to Monte Carlo, and in the Smiths' high-paying job that allows them the trappings of materialism. *Do not get sucked into this vortex.* This trait alone, unselfishness, will help keep the psychologist's bill down to a reasonable level and keep your sanity in check.

Clearly, in the end, does it really matter how many times you did the laundry vs. how many times your wife did the dishes? Are there some bonus points awarded to the one spouse that did the dishes one more time than their spouse? I would venture to say no; no one will be deciding how many bonus points are awarded to that contestant who does more of anything with one exception – those who are most unselfish win.

They win because they bring out the best in their loved ones; they bring out the best possible quality of life that is available for their family. When more than one family member is unselfish, it has a domino effect on the others; it allows all to see the bigger picture, one that ensures quality of life for all. They get infected with the unselfish virus, and for once, catching a virus is a good thing!

This awesome burden is now shared, now divided amongst the members. It becomes easier to tolerate, easier to accept, and easier to climb the mountain precisely because we are climbing it together. The disabled child wins as well as everyone else in the family. Not surprisingly, your and your spouse's stress levels decrease, and your quality of life improves.

If you can incorporate your child in all the activities your spouse and you used to do alone, everyone wins. It can be done with just a little planning and foresight and on the cheap too. Dinners out as a couple can be easily transformed into going to a local place for burgers and fries instead of a romantic evening together. Is it the same? Absolutely not, but the three of you will gain strength and bond even more closely as a family unit.

One thing to keep in mind is that you are not that dynamic anymore. The pair that has now changed to a threesome can still be as good as before; it's your responsibility to ensure it stays lively, stays important. It's a dedication one must embrace and work at constantly. It's not easy, as evidenced by the high divorce rate. So be different, be willing to change the game, and make it fun and enjoyable for each other and your child. The rules have changed, and the strategies of how to win have changed as well.

Be that spouse who knows how to create intimacy for your partner. This can take the form of a love letter, recounting a favorite memory, a small, meaningful gift, or thanking them for what they do every day. One example I can share is Laurie and I were out with a group of folks at a beach house with Derek. One of my friends mentioned "You should take your wife for a walk on the beach; we can watch Derek." We were just a phone call away if something were to happen, and we enjoyed each other's company. Seize those moments, as they are even more special in our world.

Think long term. What does my life look like in one year, five years, ten years, retirement? What can I do now to ensure my life will get better in those relative timeframes?

I'll break it down for you. In one year, which is an enormous amount of time, you should keep three things in mind: How do I make myself better, how do I better my relationship with my spouse, and how can I make my disabled child's life easier? These are written in no particular order, as the three priorities will constantly change. A good caretaker will recognize when these priorities shift and address them accordingly. Sometimes you have to better yourself to do better in your relationship with your spouse; other times it's finding a way to better your disabled child's life that will make all three priorities better.

Let's take these time horizons one at a time. In one year, some ideas could include taking a college course, learning a new skill for work or home, carving out some "me" time, seeing a therapist, or doing something charitable. Let's take each of these one at a time as well.

Taking a college course is important as it sets you in a different learning environment and capacity with young people, newer ideas, and time out from the stress of daily life. It's therapeutic. It helps in your personal and professional life. Skills from work and home are often interchangeable, and learning one can benefit so many. For example: We had a new driving technique at work that I learned, which was required for my company car. I took home the learnings and taught my wife and my daughter these same skills that made all of us safer.

Me time...the most important of all. You must find alone time to reset, re-energize, and clear your emotions and mindset. It can be a hike in the woods, a walk on the bike path, visiting a museum, or one of my favorites, getting lost for two hours in a movie theater. Most of these ideas are free or low cost, and that's important in our world. Charitable work re-grounds your thinking mind and your emotional mind. One of my favorite sayings is "someone always has it worse than you." Not only is it true, it allows your mindset to stabilize: I'm okay, I can handle this, and it provides for a good dose of empathy, something we all need.

Finally, therapy should be on everyone's menu. I'd rather change a tire every 50,000 miles than suffer a flat at 70 mph on mile 50,001. It's nothing different with therapy; it's maintenance for your mind, emotionally and figuratively. There is sadly still a stigma associated with therapy but there's no need to subscribe to that outdated theory. Help yourself so that you may help others, mainly your family. I look at therapy as just another tool in my war chest of tools needed to maintain and repair the daily damage done to my life. Without it, my life would forever be in disrepair.

The five-years-out and ten-years-out forecasts can look similar indeed for planning purposes. In five years, set goals for yourself that include long-term benefits and savings for home, life, career, and health. Take a look at your home; what can you do to both improve and save money in your household? It might be the simple, inexpensive items you can afford to do now. Maybe buy pipe insulation, caulk those drafty windows, correctly insulate your attic, or buy an efficient washer/dryer.

Money is usually a bit tighter for those with a disabled child, but these ideas are cost efficient and offer long-term benefits. There are many others, so just start with these ideas and utilize your own as well. Remember always that this is being done for your partner and your disabled child; it is the new reality. You must provide for your child, not only for your lifetime, but for his too. *Caretaking is part acceptance too.*

Life, career, and health all have values that are mutually beneficial. Staying healthy is a top priority for yourself and your family. It doesn't mean you have to look like an Adonis at the gym, but regular physical fitness improves longevity, repairs the stress on your mind, and keeps you physically flexible. When caring for your child/adult, I cannot stress this enough; as you age, physical acts become more difficult and your child will turn into an adult usually accompanied by significant weight gain. It is vital you keep yourself in the best shape possible.

Your career will be impacted favorably as well as your physical appearance, which, like it or not, is a large part of career advancement, especially in those categories of sales, servers, or customer-facing roles. Last, your confidence will improve because *nobody helps you at the gym.* Whatever gains you've made, whether it's an extra five pounds on your curls or five more minutes on the treadmill, are made because of you, no one else. You lifted the weight, you ran the extra minutes, so take pride in this and take that confidence back home with you where you will need it in making important decisions for your child and family.

Retirement time, or the decade before, which we can call pre-retirement, is fraught with some of the hardest decisions you will ever make. Who gets passed the baton for your child, where will he live, will he have enough money to be properly cared for, and will we have enough money to survive? Scary? You bet it is…you better get familiar with the term "preparation." Put yourself in that frame of mind to succeed and you will. Have a pre-retirement ten-year plan, or as I like to call it, the decade of preparation. You don't want to look back and say "I wish I'd had done that."

Mine looks like this: What am I not going to outlive in my house? Can I get those items installed and paid for before I take my dirt nap? Some examples include roofing, siding, windows, boilers, driveways, an automobile, bathroom additions, e.g., handrails, or any handicapped adjustment necessary for your child like a motorized wheelchair. If you keep your eyes on the prize and comprehend that any monies you can allocate now will help you substantially in retirement, you'll be okay. I still have a couple of items on my list to finish, but I'm well on my way to getting these done.

More important is what happens to your disabled adult once you are no longer of this planet. What becomes of him or her, and who do we entrust that responsibility to? It is an incredibly difficult question and one that becomes assumptive and presumptive at the same time.

The natural answer would be to allow your adult to live with your other children or a trusted friend. That's the presumptive part. Then the reality hits you like a Mike Tyson left hook; would I really lay this burden on someone I love? Would I want to limit and compromise my children's lives, as I know better than anyone how unselfish one has to be to survive this disability life? It is an incredibly heavy burden to carry. The extra weight of responsibility is not something many others can carry.

Most children receive an inheritance of heirlooms, monies, legacy advice, and wonderful memories when their parents pass on. Would you feel comfortable passing along the incredibly difficult assignment of caring for a disabled adult child's needs? *Caretakers find solutions.*

Our son loves to go for a ride, and ninety percent of the time all three of us go. I may be working from home, Laurie may be finishing dinner, but we all go for that ride, knowing the trip for Derek and his smile is all the reward we need. I'll finish up work when I get back from the ride, and Laurie will start dinner when we get home. It all circles back to setting priorities, asking what's really important, and being flexible.

Lots of couples would say that gaining weight is not conducive to a great relationship; in this case, gaining about 175 lbs. or so of a beautiful gift that is your disabled child is a wonderful thing. Your heart will grow as you get to bring this person along to all the venues you visited before as a couple; now it'll be one more, that's all. Take the positive; you'll get a better parking spot as that handicapped parking sticker will come in handy. In many shows we have visited, they cater to the special needs group, often giving them excellent seats and allowing an adult to sit with them.

I reminisce here about visiting The Big E in Springfield, Mass., where one of the attractions is a big top circus, and we were directed to the front of the show where Derek got to enjoy the festivities like the boss that he is! Society has come so far in recognizing these individuals with a wide variety of perks. I used to feel a bit guilty about being treated "special" with regard to my son, but I don't anymore. These kids have a hard life, and the caretakers do as well. If we as society can't allow them a brief gift of a better seat, then who are we really? Don't be held back by what easily could be called a third wheel; instead, learn how to use that wheel for better traction in your disabled child's life and your own.

Chapter 9

A Day in the Life Of

"We will either find a way or make one."

Hannibal

Perhaps a peek at a day in the life of a disabled child/adult will allow some visibility into how impactful this is to all residents of the household. Most homes have a routine where dad or mom takes their shower at night and the other takes theirs in the morning. The kids take center stage in the morning, and it's basically controlled chaos (or maybe not) in the a.m., especially in the grade school years. Contrast this with what occurs in a house with a disabled child. I can only offer a glimpse of the types of disabilities Derek has and how they impact everyone. Please take a moment to pair these moments and daily routines with yours, and you'll comprehend and be better able to use this information for your home.

My alarm goes off at six a.m., and it's time for me to get ready for work. My clothes have already been laid out on my dresser the night before including socks, shoes, and a matching belt. Sometimes I head right to the bathroom to get my routine on and am able to shave, shower, and all the rest. I'm done; time to get my boy up out of bed. He may or may not be up. He may be snoring, he may be playing the games he plays with his eyes and be in a semi-trance. He may be seizing.

I pull back his covers and am ready with his soft-sided helmet that I place over his head in case he passes out from one of his morning seizures. After some coaxing, he finally bounces up, and I place my arm under his left armpit and walk him the seven steps to the bathroom. He does his morning routine and when he's finished, we get up off the latrine, wash our hands, and placing my hand under the same armpit, escort him to the living room about twenty steps away. He sits on his couch, same spot every morning, and I open his tray table in anticipation of the breakfast he will soon eat.

My wife is up or maybe she's still sleeping, beat from the horror of yesterday's stressful events. We say good morning if she's here; if not, I turn the coffeemaker on and start to prepare breakfast for Derek and myself. Laurie has either pre-made French toast or I make him some waffles. His cup and our coffee cups are sitting on the stove top, pre-made the night before with Carnation Instant Breakfast for Derek and with sugar in our cups of soon-to-be-delicious hot coffee.

I check and the waffles are done in the toaster oven, and I bring them out to my main man, topped with maple syrup but not too much as he hates getting his fingers sticky. Laurie is up, and I say morning to her and give her the cup of coffee she is pining for. I grab my oatmeal and cup of Joe and flip open my iPad to see what awaits me in the business world. I read my emails, set my day, finish my bowl and cup, and more often than not, empty the dishwasher. My wife is now alert after the caffeine kicks in and is ready for another scheduled day of not knowing what the heck is going to happen.

After kissing my wife and my boy, I leave for work, and I always let her know that she should call me if she needs me. My day is off to a start, and I know that I will have an end. At some point today my job will be finished. I'll make that last sales call, finish my last spreadsheet, and take that last conference call. I will be *done.* I work hard, I make decent money, and it's both motivating and rewarding. Tomorrow will start a new workday and at the end of that day, I'll be done too.

My wife does not have that same luxury. Her day can be planned and if she's lucky, it'll be the one day out of a hundred where it will go that way. Her day is never done. Observation of Derek alone uncovers new things seemingly every week at times. How long has he been doing that behavior? Does he look like he's in pain to you? Is it time to accelerate or reduce his next new medication? The questions are nearly endless, and the thought processes behind them can go on like a bad dream. There is no end, no finality, no marker that says "Laurie, you are now finished." Days roll into weeks, months roll into and out of seasons, and Laurie is still on call, still on duty 24/7.

Laurie starts her day in earnest; what's in store for me today, she asks her inner self? Will Derek be good, will he have a bad day, will I be able to check off a host of lists I've been meaning to do?

It's now past eight and he has been fed and medicated, and my wife has brushed his teeth, applied his deodorant, washed him, dressed him, shaved him, sprayed him with his cologne, and combed his hair. She finishes with a flourish, asking Derek "Who's the most handsome boy?" He reacts with a smile, a laugh, and his physical gesture of hands up around his shoulders fists slightly clenched. He might playfully hit his mother in the arm to show his love. If it's a good day, she might get a kiss on the lips and be greeted with that wild-eyed look of "Did I just do that?" Momma will smile and say thanks for that, Derek! It's amazing for me to witness on the weekends.

We think Derek is part Romanian, as we suspect he has vampire blood running through his veins. He doesn't sleep well through the night, and his modus operandi is to catch up on his sleep in the morning hours on his couch. Oftentimes he will sleep for a couple of hours uninterrupted, and those are the days my wife cherishes. It's about the best case scenario for Derek to start his day. No seizures usually during his sleep periods, and he wakes up refreshed, another prerequisite for helping to eliminate seizure activity. On those days, the sun shines a little brighter, the stress levels are a little less, and Momma Wilk has much better days.

Then there are those days you wish upon no one. It usually starts the day before with some suspect behavior on Derek's part. He will be "alive," a little too ramped up and out of his regular routine. We catch a glimpse of how life could be as he is closer to how a normal child would act like during these times. Unfortunately, the omen has been revealed, and it's a harbinger of what's to come. We wait for the other shoe to drop in the form of increased seizure activity, or more violent seizures, or both.

Neither is easy to observe, and they're a disappointing reminder that this is Derek's life, and ours. He didn't ask for these seizures and certainly didn't do anything to deserve them, but still here we are. This predictor of behavior is eerily accurate and being prepared is all we can do.

The powers of attentiveness are on high alert; we watch him intently for any of the "tells" that come with impending seizure activity. We make bathroom trips with me holding him even tighter than usual, so most of his physical activity is quieted. His specialized medication that stops his seizures, should they not cease on their own, is available and ready for use at a moment's notice. Once administered, Midazolam works quite quickly, usually in a few minutes' time, and Derek will often sleep for a couple of hours. It allows for a reset of the activity that causes seizures, and we are thankful to have a tool like this at our disposal.

These are the days that knock the wind out of our sails. I suppose we are a bit immune to seeing our child seize, but it's never a sight that we get used to. All we can do is comfort him, rub his head, tell him we love him, and wrap him with a blanket. When Derek comes to, he probably feels like you or I do after taking a heavy-duty sleeping pill. He is clearly out of sorts and wobbly on his feet the first time he stands. Those lists Laurie would like to accomplish ain't happening today….

Remember that part I spoke about helping your partner out? Invariably the call will come from Laurie, "Honey, can you pick up Derek's medication, a loaf of bread, milk?" "Yes dear, I will." This now takes precedence over whatever I had on my list of things to do. *Remain flexible and positive.* I tell myself a couple of things during these trying times; I reset back to basics. The questions I ask are "Am I healthy, do I have a job, do I have a home and a wife and a family?"

The answer, of course, to all these questions is affirmative, and I feel better about myself and our situation. It's a habit I highly recommend to all the caretakers who have had their bad days. Someone always has it worse than you.

Our aide comes over to assist Derek with his OT and PT. Cindy is a former teacher and a longtime friend of Laurie's who Derek has been working with for a few years now. On good days, when the little man isn't sleeping or seizing, she can get some work done with him. She keeps him busy with word games, multiplication tables, puzzles, and coloring books.

On the PT side, Laurie has done a great job securing a custom-built walker for Derek, and he will walk around the living room to get some exercise. Living in the Northeast creates some outdoor activity challenges during the winter, but we live just a couple hundred feet from a bike path and when the weather cooperates, the girls take Derek for a walk/carriage ride down the path. They will walk him for a bit until he signals all done and then he gets to see Coventry in his carriage. When Derek cooperates and the weather doesn't, we also have a bike pedal machine he can use indoors for exercise.

It's relevant to note that there are multiple ways to solve for physical activity for a disabled child/adult; these are just what work for us. Be creative and include other ideas. Perhaps your child/adult is more physically able, so you could get a gym membership or sign up at your local YMCA. Physical activity is so important for everyone's mental health, and trust me: With what is going on in our world, we can use all the help we can get in that area. I implore all to engage in this type of activity; if you're healthy and your doctor says it's okay, what's the downside?

The rest of Laurie's day looks something like this: Fill all medication vials, count out and gather all pills that are to be dispensed, check online to see when the next prescriptions are available for pick-up, and coordinate with the multiple doctors to authorize for future refills. She will, of course, clean the house and prep for Derek's lunch and the family's dinner. She will also assist in taking Derek for toiletry purposes, wash his hands, and walk him back to the couch.

When outside activities are called for, Laurie must put a plan together for trips to Walmart, CVS, or Derek's dentist/doctor appointments as well as her own. She tries to get all this done with her aide to minimize the safety issue for Derek. If our aide is sick or has a day off unexpectedly, her plans are changed and new days/times are scheduled. She does not get the opportunity to live a stress-free scheduled life.

It's an ever-changing landscape she must navigate and flexibility is always the key word. Here's another key point to consider when delegating roles to each spouse. Laurie is a day-to-day thinker, and I've always been a long-term one. It only occurred to me recently why she is so short term. *She has to be.* It's at the core of her everyday routine. Her day changes so quickly she must be both nimble enough and prepared enough to react accordingly.

I've always been the long-term guy. Being male, working for a large company, and my own upbringing have fostered this approach. Males are programmed to be the man, to provide for a safe haven, and to establish that retirement nest egg. Here's your teachable moment; *We balance one another yet again.* It's a thought that should be kept top of mind; keep the relationship balanced for both caretakers and, of course, your disabled child. *Caretaking is a balancing act for all.*

I come home from work and ask Laurie how her day and how Derek's day was. I am prepared for multiple answers. Was it a good day, was it bad, did he have many seizures? Sometimes I can tell by the lack of makeup or what she is wearing that today wasn't the best day for the Derek or her. If the morning dishes are still in the sink, this means Derek required all the time available for that day and that's okay. I'll take care of the dishes and spend more time with Derek, if possible.

Instead of us talking about what he did at school, I find out about how many types of seizures he had for the day, or if he didn't, how nice of a surprise today was. See, we have names for these seizures like all families do, and Laurie has a book detailing all his seizure activity, what time, what day, how many, and his reactions.

These are our conversation pieces; instead of how did Derek do on his science test, we talk about these things all disabled families talk about and that's okay too. Instead of worrying about his next project at school being completed, we worry about his medications and hope he will get better. We advocate for our child. The conversation isn't much different, because it centers on interest and wanting what is best for our child.

I never come home and ask my wife if Derek is disabled. I ask how his day was because I care about him as much as everyone does who has a child in an Honors class. Do you think these people come home and say "Gee, honey, is our kid intelligent?" Maybe they do, but I bet the first words out of their mouth are the same as ours; how is my child doing today? And that is what counts, my friends. *Be grateful for your interest in your child.*

It can be challenging and difficult to engage in activities with your disabled child/adult. Nothing is the same from day to day with these little bundles of joy, and you never know what will happen from one minute to the next. This doesn't give us an excuse not to try to engage them in some type of suitable behavior based around their skillset, however. In our case, Derek doesn't have a lot of hobbies or anything he is truly interested in other than his rides in the car. It can be very hard to engage him on days when he just doesn't want to be bothered. *Caretaking is accepting what cannot be changed.*

Of particular note is the loneliness a caretaker can feel when in charge of a disabled child. There can be feelings of desperation, anxiety, a "me against the world" categorization of one's life. Don't let these feelings get in the way of caring for your child. They are perfectly normal, and I'd be more worried for you if you didn't feel this way from time to time. It's a lot to handle on a day-to-day basis. When you realize what you're up against in this lifestyle, sometimes you'll have bad days and that's okay.

To use a baseball analogy, a .300 hitter is considered to be an elite batter. This means he also fails seven out of ten times. But the good hitters are always practicing, always learning, and never giving up. You will have those days where you felt like you went hitless in five at-bats. Get up the next day and swing away; good things happen to those who don't quit. And we have something far more valuable than a baseball to care for at our home park.

Once our aide leaves, Laurie and Derek will take a short nap to refresh. If he's having a bad day seizure-wise, it's best to let him rest and recover. On days when he wants to engage, he will tolerate playing catch until he throws the ball as far away from you as humanly possible. Normally, he has incredible aim, and this signifies he's all done with you and the ball! Derek also likes to be outside, and we will oblige, dressing him appropriately and sitting at our outdoor café. Sometimes he's interested in nature and sometimes not. It's okay. We are experiencing it together, and it's better than lying on the couch taking up space. *Make the best of the situation.* Caretaking is being innovative.

It's nine p.m., and I initiate the process of getting Derek ready for bed. The preparation has already started for his safety and my ease of transition to his dreamland. I have turned down his bed, turned on his TV, placed toothpaste on his toothbrush, and opened the toilet seat.

I let him know it's time for bed, he gets up, I place his helmet on him, and I walk him towards the bathroom. In yet another quirk indigenous to our world, somehow Derek has acquired the knowledge to look back upon entry to the bathroom and induce a seizure. These are the type that will drop him to the ground. It's something I have to be on guard for, and Laurie never lets me forget: "Don't let him look back!" He tries, I grab his helmet so he can't, and crisis averted. A heightened sense of awareness is a necessity for this life.

He takes care of business on the throne and while he is sitting, I brush his teeth. He reluctantly allows me access to the inside of his mouth, so I can clean that part of his pearly whites and rinse his mouth out the best I can. I ask him if he is done, and he gets up, we take off his sweatpants, he flushes the toilet, and we wash our hands. I walk him to his bed, he lies down, and I take his helmet off.

He has this repetitive behavior where after he lies down, he must get up again into the sitting position, and rub his head, and he can then lie back down. This can be problematic as his pass-out seizures seem to happen more frequently at this time, and he runs the risk of falling out of bed. I stand in the hallway just out of sight, as I haven't been able to break him of this habit. Once I'm satisfied he is finished, I move along.

Laurie will finish the day that was by giving him his final medications at ten p.m. She will say prayers with Derek and lie down and cuddle with him. This is a special time for her and son as she asks for Derek's well-being from her higher power and her day will finish with a well-earned good night's sleep. It's another day we have both entered into the record books.

We have survived our pitfalls, done the best possible job that we could have, and tomorrow is another day to be conquered. Another of my favorite sayings is "Make the best decision based on the information available at that time." Second-guessing will lead to sleepless nights and a guaranteed poor performance the following day.

"Finish each day and be done with it. You have done what you could. Some blunders and absurdities no doubt crept in; forget them as soon as you can. Tomorrow is a new day. You shall begin it serenely and with too high a spirit to be encumbered with your old nonsense."
— Ralph Waldo Emerson

I have prepared this day and night routine for him for many reasons. Safety is of a primary concern and is at the top of the list. The absolute last thing I need to complicate this routine is not being prepared and allowing for idle time during any of these processes. The less idle time Derek has, the less time for a seizure, the less possibility of him hurting himself. I highly recommend this process or one like it to everyone.

Here's why. If you aren't making preparations for him when you have the time, you won't be prepared for all the extraneous duties we all have when caring for a disabled child/adult. The random phone call, the inevitable wearing out of an appliance, the normal forgetfulness we all experience in our day-to-day routine will all become bigger problems than they need to be if you can't take care of your child.

Let time work for you; it can easily be done with a little fore-sight. Let the dishes soak for fifteen minutes before you wash them, use that time to get the load of wash going or place that next load into the dryer. While that's working for you, preheat the oven for dinner. Reduce the possibility of as many surprises as you can, because as we all know, they seem to come at us quicker and in higher volume than in normal households. Preempt those surprises; you'd be shocked as to how much you can actually control both time-wise and chore-wise.

As the day ends and with sleepy eyes, make sure to give thanks for the life you lead. One of the easiest ways is to tell your spouse that you love them. It means so much more in our family dynamic than in most others; the love we are stating is for so much more than just each other. It's for all the seizures Derek has that Laurie must cope with. It's for all the meals she cooks that I consume. Those meals that are prepared no matter how bad D's day gets or what emotional firestorm has engulfed my wife that particular day.

The "I love you" is for picking me up when I'm down, doing my ledger of chores when I have a bad day, and doing the most difficult job on the planet: mothering a disabled child, sacrificing so much, and loving him with all her heart. I get to love her and love the love she radiates towards Derek. That's an awful lot of love, and I'm grateful and humbled to have this experience. Ending the day with a grateful heart makes it easier to wake up with one.

I wrote this poem for my son's twenty-fourth birthday, and I thought I'd share it with all of you. It comes straight from my heart, and I think it encompasses many of the same thoughts we as special needs parents have deep within our collective psyches. I hope you find your child in the words also.

Dreamin' of D

Does life's laughter come in his dreams?

Does his smile crease his thoughts?

Do the chains fall away when he slumbers?

Crashing to the ground in silence.

Is he free from the weight of his albatrosses?

Does he find flight and weightlessness?

And can he run free on the wings of a warm breeze

And claim joy while his freedoms last?

Are friends available for him

To joke with, to get an ice cream cone

The kind that drips on a hot summer day

And ruins your favorite shirt?

In his dreams does he play quarterback?

Or maybe he's a lineman holding down the fort.

Is he in the game of his life?

Is sorrow felt as equally as the feeling of rejoice?

Would his loves be those born with blonde locks?

Or is he a fan of the darker side?

Will he make passes at girls with glasses?

Or is his type sporty or perhaps country?

While he sleeps are his thoughts of school

Or perhaps what lunchbox he would like to show off?

Is it Spiderman, Superman, or a Ninja Turtle?

Mom, can I have PB & J for lunch?

I like the way you make it.

What lights his eyes up when he speaks to mom?

Is it algebra or chemistry perhaps literature

Chaucer or Thoreau, Einstein, or Tesla?

Is his favorite color blue or red or the entire prism?

Does he find his pot o' gold at the end of his rainbow?

In his escape, does he know the emotions?

Does he know the fears of love and a first kiss?

The ask of a lady's hand at the prom?

And does he navigate successfully

The politics of cliques and fraternities?

Does he revel in acing his biology test?

Or in knowing who was the first World Series MVP?

Unshackled, does he see the world like we do

In all its beauty and does he discover new things?

Those that light up his world and excite his senses

Like we do?

As he drifts off, is he safe in his knowledge

That his parents and family love him

And that this blanket will keep him warm

For eternity and beyond?

D, do you dream of what I hope for you?

Tell me your color, your girl, your team.

Or you can keep it a secret I'm okay with that.

And let my imagination run

Unencumbered in my love for you.

And I can smile at you and you at me

And we both will know the truth.

Brian Wilk

Chapter 10

Raising a Child Normally vs Disabled

"You can't always get what you want."

The Rolling Stones

It's hard to raise a child in today's world; it takes real effort and real responsibility. It takes your best day every day; it takes having zero sick days, zero vacations, and no personal days. It takes efforts of Herculean proportions to be successful at this endeavor. Collectively, it takes a teacher, it takes a cook, a nurse, a mathematician, and it takes everything you've been taught by your parents. But then we need one more discipline; you must then add your own ingredients into the mix! The experience you need for this job? It comes after the test, these lessons....

These ingredients are different for everyone. All of us have been brought up with differing sets of values, morals, ethics, and guidance. Our parents have brought a different set of values to the table when they decided to raise us. They spoke with each other; they in turn decided what would be kept from their parents and what was to be discarded. Sometimes, actually quite often, certain tendencies remain no matter how hard our parents try to eliminate them.

These tendencies are what personify us at our very core, at our center. They're what makes a Johnson, a Johnson; a Smith, a Smith. They're the way we walk, talk, and speak. They're our mannerisms and our thought patterns. Our parents left us a blueprint, and whether it trickles down to us through diffusion or osmosis, what's left is what we see in the mirror every day, each one of us.

We must pay attention to these little idiosyncrasies, let go of what doesn't really matter, and keep the important stuff. This is different for each couple, and the equation for success thus is different for each couple. It almost always boils down to what is good for the disabled member of the family versus what's most important to the couple or the individual parent.

There are so many different ways to perform a chore. What you've learned is one way, a way. It doesn't make it absolute or even correct. So take the fact that you like to do dishes a different way from your wife, and throw that crap out the window. It doesn't matter! What does matter is that you do the dishes if she doesn't. She changes the oil in the car if you don't. Stuff gets done and the gender-bending that takes place along the way is of zero consequence. Be unisexual, start a fad....

The divisor is two. Take all the chores and divide them in two equal piles; some days your pile is higher, just do those chores anyway. Sometimes it's less; give thanks to your spouse when this day ends. Consequentially, I don't mind at all being the laundry person in my house. You know, my wife once YouTubed a video on how to replace a carburetor on our lawnmower. She didn't tell me she was going to do it; she just sent me a video on my cell phone at work stating "Laurie's Small Engine Repair" gets the job done!

This particular day is very busy for me at work. I'm jammed, and I get the text from my wife. I open my phone, and I see my wife, tools in hand, grease on her fingers, smiling and saying she fixed the mower. I smiled too, shaking my head muttering to myself, "Leave it to my wife." This is yet another example of doing what needs to be done and performing those tasks so that your loved one doesn't have to. She fixed the mower, I didn't, and who cares? She never once rubbed it in my face, degrading me for not being a "real" man. Again, no gender, just doing what needed to be done. She just did it out of love, for me and for Derek. That's what it takes for a disabled family to succeed: a total team effort.

I cannot overstate this fact enough. There are dozens of chores that need to be done on a daily, weekly, and monthly basis. If you leave them for your spouse to do, this will lead to bad news. Both of you have a difficult job in rearing a disabled child; show them that you love them by doing an extra chore or two. Think of it this way; doing an extra chore will save you a trip to the florist!

It's pretty obvious, isn't it, that my wife fixing the lawnmower went a long way in my mind? I'm not sure about which brand I chose, but years later I bought her a ride-on mower. Yes, I said I bought her that. She let me know that if I bought it, she would do the lawn. Somewhere back in that dark area of my mind I was probably able to recall that she took the time to fix the old lawnmower, and that she should get what she wanted for a ride-on. Leave it to Laurie; she wanted one with a cup holder for her beer!

It's just an example of give and take; that's all it really is. I look at this situation that we're in and know that we need to be all in, one hundred percent all in. If we both are able to give sixty percent, it should be an easier ride for the two of us initially, and by default will allow us to spend more time with our beloved Derek. Everybody wins! It's like you're at the carnival: Step right up, everybody is a winner! It's how life should be lived, with happiness, optimism, gratitude, and a general sense of recognizing the good fortune you have. I never want my family or myself to feel depressed or live life under a constant cloud. That would be a life wasted, and since I don't believe in reincarnation, it would also be tragic. We get one ride, so make your tickets count.

Throughout my life, I've had some difficult jobs; I also like to excel at whatever I do. Once again, my past has come back to help as the long-term goal is always about Derek and how we solve for him. The equation must always have Derek as the primary solve. Any dividends from any solutions we have can then be administered to Laurie, me, and the rest of our family. Unselfish love is hard to come by, but the quicker the family embraces this type of love, the better the results for all.

Now take all this loving, teaching, nursing, and responsibility and administer this to a disabled child. You can do these things to a child under normal circumstances, and you will invariably receive some type of reward for performing these duties admirably. You'd expect to receive the hug, the smile, a high five, a misty-eyed look perhaps. And you'd be right. Love has been taught to us as a two-way street – you get what you give, although not equally all the time – but in the long run it should even out.

Not so with a disabled child. It's not that they don't want to; they can't, and we keep hoping this will change, that somehow someone out there in Fairytale land will spread the magic dust and that our child will be cured. Your child will show love sometimes; the smile, the tears, the look…but today it doesn't come and you are left with yet another decision. Do I continue to show love without any payback; do I continue to do the things that a responsible parent should do?

In your mind, you know, of course, it's the right thing to do, but in actuality it is a disturbing void, one that doesn't come with a manual to read, or a tutor to help you decipher what to do and what not to do. It only comes from within, from your heart and from the hearts of your family.

In our family, it comes from the heart of Derek. It is he who holds the manual, he who becomes our tutor, he who shows us the way. It is painful, the steps are excruciatingly slow and seemingly lead to nowhere, or at least to a place that we've never been to before. And that is exactly the point; you must extend yourself into places where you are not comfortable.

It is after all a place where Derek will reside for the rest of his life; the least we can do is join him there. Allow yourselves the freedoms to expand your definition of a family and life. *Que sera, sera* is often a good saying to fall back on when feelings of hopelessness occurs. Stay positive, keep smiling, and good things will happen.

Inclusion is a hot topic in today's corporate world and in present-day society. By definition, to be inclusive is to include others regardless of their differences. Johnny is African-American; that's cool, and he can come join us. Mary is a blind person; okay, Mary, welcome to the group. As hard as it is to include others in your group that are of equal intellect and who may look or act differently, imagine how hard it must be to include a child with a disability into a group setting. Here's the difference; we can see that Johnny is black and identify him as of a different race. Nearly always, blindness is overt or is communicated to us verbally. We can see, touch, or feel the difference.

Again, it isn't so with disabled children. How many times has the question been asked by someone viewing your disabled child who may be ignorant or impolite: What's wrong with your child? Let's break this down too. If a child is in a wheelchair, that's usually a good clue he is disabled. Might be temporary like a sprained ankle or knee, but most of the time it signifies a disability. *But which one?*

The average person has no idea what this child has for a disability. There is a general feeling of empathy for the fact that he is disabled but no targeted knowledge of what the affliction is. Take Mary, for instance; we can tell she's blind and understand what it's like not to see. We can certainly put ourselves in her place. Maybe not with full knowledge, but close enough to feel empathy for her *particular* situation. That's a huge difference in understanding one's situational disability.

We are taught from a very young age what a person of different color looks like, because it's obvious, or what makes a heterosexual different from a homosexual. It's a common conversation these days as it should be. But ask a child to explain the difference between Asperger's and Parkinson's, mental retardation versus Tourette's, and I bet they'd get it wrong more than they'd get it right.

It's *still* a taboo subject that is not talked about frequently or easily. Why? In our encounters with humans, it's natural to expect you'd meet up with normal folks. You've met them before; you know how they react to certain situations.

As a child it's still the same. If you meet up with another child, the normal greeting of "hi" would most probably be met with a reciprocal hello. It's not so easy when met with indifference, a violent outburst, or an inappropriate response. It is as uncomfortable a situation as there could be for a child. They do not know what the issue is with this strange human. They will ask mommy or daddy "Why does that little boy not like me?"

Mommy is uncomfortable too and doesn't want to say the wrong thing in this politically correct world of ours for fear of hurting the disabled child's feelings. It's simply the lack of normalcy that makes this interaction so tedious. It's up to us as caretakers to educate and diffuse the circumstances, so that the next interaction is a positive one for all involved.

It's because as parents and society in general, we have not done a great job of educating our children about the various conditions people have. Give this some thought too; disability is highly unmarketable. It's why it doesn't receive any press. It's overbearing, depressing, and a chore to acknowledge such abnormalities. It's also disconcerting for that thought to surface as a parent for a couple of reasons. I don't want *my* child to be burdened by the thought of someone suffering so much and "What if that was my child?" We want normal kids; nearly everyone does. It's why it's so hard to be inclusive with disabled children; it conjures up depression, an uneasy sadness for the parents and the person with the disability. It knocks people down a peg or two, and it's very uncomfortable to witness.

Still more factors to consider when being inclusive: How is Jimmy going to get up that hill with his wheelchair? How is Jane going to play volleyball with her oxygen tank? The point is this: Let the parents of the child and even the child himself make that decision. You'd be surprised as to how nimble someone can be in a wheelchair! Hey, they have more experience in that environment than you do; *give them a chance.*

What about Jane's oxygen tank? She may not need it all the time, and most games can be altered to let a child with a disability play and feel as if they are part of a group. Here's a novel idea: ASK! Just ask what the needs are of that particular person and accommodate that person and the group. You'll be

doing way more good than you think. That child gets to participate and feel loved, the parents feel joy as well, and your
offspring will be taught a valuable life lesson going forward.
Another example to be placed in the win/win column!

If your child is ambulatory, in good physical health, and a doctor
has signed off on him participating in strenuous physical
activity, take a hard look at Special Olympics. So many good
things can come out of this for a child and a parent. It boosts
your child's confidence, gives him a sense of satisfaction, and
will surely put a smile on his face. I can't imagine a child's
elation at winning a race or the pride a parent must feel when
their child excels against the competition.

Another positive that comes out of these engagements is
valuable knowledge from your peers about issues they may
have faced and solved for. It will also build a sense of
community and camaraderie that you won't find elsewhere. The
networking you'll experience here will only be a positive for you
and your child. I wholeheartedly endorse exposure to these
types of events. Your local school or YMCA may have similar
types of sports gatherings and if you can't get to the Special
Olympics, these are suitable options. Matriculate into society;
you'll be glad you did.

Pat yourself on the back as a parent. You've done two great
things and for that alone you should feel great; however, the
lesson will be taught going forward by your child who will share
this with his friends. Down the road, don't be surprised if your
child leads a committee, gets involved in a cause, or becomes
an HR professional because of a teachable moment such as this.
You can be that person who starts the chain, you can change
the world, and it's up to you and your attitude, choosing your
course wisely.

We've been lucky to reside on a street where there were about six families who had kids plus or minus two years from our own kids. They all played together and spent time at each other's houses. They competed in pickup games and sports of various types, and I give them an above-average grade for including everyone in the group. When the games or sports happened to be played in our house's backyard, I would change my grade to an A plus.

I can't ever think of a time where they did not want to include Derek, and for the most part the prompting did not come from us as parents; it came from the kids themselves. You'd be genuinely surprised at how inclusive kids can be today. Maybe it's my time spent in the corporate world and all the valuable training I received, or maybe society has embraced this as a trickle-down effect. Whatever the reasons, I'm thrilled that I witnessed it in my own circle of friends and neighbors and continue to witness it in my travels outside of my neighborhood. *Caretaking is coaching inclusivity.*

Here's how you can win at this inclusion game: be authentic. You are never too old to learn. Here's a little lesson I learned at age twenty-six or so. I owned a Tropicana route in the RI area, and every Friday I would start out delivering to the East Side and finish on Broad Street. Every Friday for the first three weeks, I'd run out of apple juice on Broad Street. Finally, I asked a couple of the store owners, why do you sell so much apple juice? Once they told me that apple juice was the favorite of Spanish folks, I understood why.

The East Side was filled with college kids and is probably in the top five neighborhoods in the state in terms of Caucasian population; orange juice was king there. That's not the case on

Broad Street, which is home to one of the highest per capita Dominican populations in the country.

José from Providence Market, who took a liking to me, provided me with the initial information about this, and I never ran out of apple juice again. Had he not been inclusive with me and vice versa, it would have taken me much longer to get this fixed. I learned something valuable from José, and getting my mix of products correct for the demographic I served was the lesson of a lifetime. I was also able to pick up many bodegas because I learned a bit of Spanish to help with the ordering process; I can tell you it was very much appreciated by my customers and separated me from the competition.

Separate yourself from the competitive forces in life too. The goal is not to be better than your neighbors next door, down the street, or in other neighborhoods. The goal should be to get better within yourself, within your family, and most important for your disabled child. Chasing materialism will often hinder any chance you have of making a better life for your child.

Whatever money you may have that is disposable should clearly be allocated towards the betterment of your child, now and into the future. Instead of money, use the value of a sunny day to have a picnic with the family, or rejoice in the latest accomplishment of your child, or equally as important, a skill you recently learned and are mastering. Discipline of self and self-growth are two tenets not to be overlooked. Once again, stay positive, rejoice in life's moments, and be grateful.

Chapter 11

Self-Doubt, Confidence, and Overcoming Your Fears

"If you hear a voice within you say 'you cannot paint,' then by all means paint and that voice will be silenced."

Vincent Van Gogh

The self-doubt: There are days that come out of nowhere, out of some hidden darkness that sometimes builds to that maddening crescendo. Sometimes it just happens, but they come, uninvited and unwelcome. Those are days that take your breath away, days that suck the sunshine and the optimism right out of you like the feeling of the top scoop of ice cream falling just out of your grasp on the hottest July afternoon. Those days where you want to stay in bed, stay under the covers, no lights, just darkness, and just chill in your mind. No thoughts, no activity, just a serene blankness that can take the place of reality.

But like a tide that rises twice a day, you have to find the strength, you have to find the motivation to carry on. And it's not for you, sunshine; it's for your child, for your disabled child. For us, it's for Derek and his love, his sometimes unrequited love. It's for the day he looks at us and smiles or blows a kiss. It's that bonus time, that too-infrequent time when he seems almost normal, and we catch a glimpse of what might have been.

That's why we get up, why we cast aside the covers, why we trade the serenity of the blank canvas that would be our mind that day for the stress of the day at hand. We know it's coming, like a car wreck in slow motion, yet there we are standing tall and waving to no one in particular and barely audibly saying

"Bring it on; I got you." It's for Derek, not for us, not ever for us, and that is what we call love Derek's love. And it's worth it; every single day it's worth it.

Know your role; there is a family dynamic that takes place when you receive a disabled child into your life. It is nearly impossible for both parents to work under the extremely stressful conditions naturally present. This means each parent must take part in a pact, one where the division of duties is both clear and muddied at the same time.

Our activities are often disturbed or put off because of the randomness of our disabled children's issues. They may have a seizure, they may have to go to the bathroom after having just gone fifteen minutes before, or maybe they've fallen asleep at just the time you wanted to do some shopping.

To make the best of your time, a concept that no one can get extra of, do the things that can be done right then and there. If there are dishes in the sink, do them; if laundry needs to be folded, fold like you've never folded before. Here's why: When that unforeseen event happens, that seizure, that bathroom trip, you want to eliminate as much noise as you can to keep the stressors that you can control down to a manageable level. *Control the stressors as much as possible.*

A primary caretaker and a primary wage earner must be appropriated when at all possible. It is unfortunate and inefficient to expect both parents to work and both to experience the stressors present in this environment. I've always stated that the reason why our marriage has been successful is because of what I call the division of fifty dimensions that make a great partnership. If there are indeed fifty dimensions that make a good marriage, my wife is clearly queen of the dimensions I truly suck at. The same is true of the reverse; it is precisely why we flourish in this partnership.

My trust in her doing the things she does well is unshakeable. Here's a thought: Who likes to do things they suck at? Who likes to do things they are good at? The answer is straightforward; do the things you do well, leave the things you do not do so well to your partner. Trust in them as much as you trust in yourself to get these things done. You owe them that and they owe you that as well. If you equally suck at a couple of dimensions, pick each other up, figure it out, talk it out, and be respectful of the stressors you each face in your daily lives. Above all, do not be selfish. Fight for your team, not for individual honors. The team always performs best when everyone is on the same page and the give is for the team, for Derek, for the long haul.

My career calling was probably in finance; for whatever reason numbers always came easy to me, so I am the captain of retirement planning in my house. I explain the reasons for doing what I do to my wife, but after twenty-nine years of marriage, you can tell she doesn't have the best grasp of this, nor does she want to. I always took care of this.

She *trusts* me for doing this the right way, the way that will afford us a best shot at a reasonable retirement. She knows, without saying, that I'm doing this for us and not me. Ask me the last time I wrote a check. I haven't written one in twenty-nine years, and still no bounced checks. No need to confirm. I trust my wife to make the right decisions.

Conversely, my parenting skills are not on a par with my financial skills. My wife, I think, wrote the book on being a great parent, a great mother. A CEO if you will of parenting. She has this thing called patience. I was not so familiar with that word in my early days. Exasperation came pretty easy to me. I should not have been put in charge of that department, and I wasn't.

I deferred most of the parenting skills, and skills are very clearly what they are, to my princess of patience. I knew she could do a better job in her sleep than I could on my own. Call it whatever you want – swallowing one's ego, being submissive, doing what is right for the family – it's what has made us successful in raising our disabled child and other children. Recall that I had a child from a previous marriage, which only added to the difficulty of our family. No worries, Laurie handled that too. Caretaking is being flexible and being part of a team.

What to do when either parent is at odds with a given discipline? Laurie asked me very early on in our courtship how we would raise our children with respect to religion. My wife is very religious; I am not. I deferred to her, saying she could raise them her way, and that I would let our children know the way I feel when they were old enough to make a decision. This is a hard area for any two people to agree on, let alone two married folks with polar opposite views. *Seeking a solution is Caretaking 101.*

It's exactly this type of give-and-take that is so important in being successful at raising any children, never mind with the added challenges of raising a child with a disability. Always try to take the path that leads to less damage. Sometimes not being what you think is right is the correct answer. It's a bit of a lost art to think in the perspective of another, especially if it impacts a disabled child. My hat is truly off to my wife who has done yeoman's work in raising our whole family.

One of the themes that you will recognize as being repetitive in this book is my praise for others; none of us are in this alone, we all depend on each other for existence. Recall that I'll still get a phone call randomly from my wife giving thanks to me for letting her stay home and raise her children. One of the immediate benefits of this call is that it puts a pep in my step, and an extra beat in my heart as I know the person I have been providing for with my hard work has recognized me for it. Maybe some husbands would get mad for having to work to provide for the whole family, and that's unfortunate. What truly matters is the sanctity of the family.

Derek naturally received the most attention growing up; he required it. Put a slightly different way: Would you continue teaching someone after they got the concept you were showing them? Or would you move on to either another concept or spend more time with a child who hasn't quite gotten the hang of it?

There's a saying: Fairness doesn't mean everyone gets what they want, it means everyone gets what they need. Communication and explanation are two pillars that hold this tenet truthful. The question did come up from Haley, "Mommy, why do you spend so much time with Derek?" Mommy had to be truthful and communicative, and explain that her brother needed some extra time, because we all learn at different speeds.

Perhaps the best way to illustrate this is by bringing up a situation where the questioning sister may have had a harder time than normal in learning a new discipline. Mother may say, "Do you remember when Mommy spent some extra time with you so that you could learn how to say that new word?" The light bulb should go off; if not try another way, find another way.

Laurie would defuse that seemingly unfair prejudice shown to Derek with having girls' nights with Haley. They would watch a movie in Haley's room, complete with popcorn, blankets, and lots of love. They would talk girls' talk, the type of stuff we guys just don't get. The type of stuff that is insignificant to an outsider. These special times would form the bonds that they share to this day.

My daughter is now twenty-six and on her way in life. The reason she is on her way is because her mother took the time during those talks to show her how to get there. She taught her all the ways to be a woman, a good citizen, how to have empathy, how to be friends with everyone. Laurie was an HR expert long before either she or Haley knew of the term. To this very day, our house fills with the United Nations of peoples as Haley is friends with everyone. It may be my proudest moment as a family man.

This is so important in today's world. 'Murica is called the Melting Pot for good reason; we opened our borders to nearly all countries in the 1800s. Now, there are double the countries, and this melting pot has mixed morals, ethics, and customs to a whole other varied complexion. A successful friend and worker must be able to understand and relate to many belief systems, and being exposed to this as a young person does something wonderful; it frames your persona into a "this is normal" as a matter of course. It defines cultural inclusion and acceptance and fosters the spirit of cooperation, something that is needed in abundance in a family with a disabled child. *Caretaking is being inclusive and accepting.*

I *never* felt neglected as a husband, and Laurie is to be credited for that. There are only twenty-four hours in everyone's day, and she made the most of them, giving love where needed and in the correct dosages. It's a credit to her that none of us ever felt left out of anything. The queen of caretaking resides in my castle.

At the time of my daughter's grade school/high school days, I was delivering products for Tropicana. This would require me to be in contact with hundreds of customers. I'll tell you a great story about that. I had a boss who was very demanding and who pushed us all to the limits of sanity. He had a scorecard at the warehouse where everyone had their posted totals by day for the week. If you had the audacity to come in below your goal, watch out. It would get loud in a hurry. This man should go on a motivational speaking tour.

He and I had a contentious relationship at best when we first started working together. See, my route was just that, mine, and I worked independently of Tropicana for the most part. This guy came in with a Pharaoh complex and thought we would all build a pyramid for him. It didn't help matters that he was six feet seven inches tall!

The underlying context here is that we needed someone like him, someone who would kick our butt; otherwise, our system, which was in its infancy, could certainly fail. This man is responsible for me writing this book. He and I had a conversation about Derek before Derek's latest operation, and he said some very poignant words to me. He said, "Brian, with what you and Laurie have been through, I bet there'd be many people who would want to hear your story and how you stay so positive given your situation." I pretty much told him to shut up, but he wouldn't get off the subject.

It was like he knew before I did that this would help many people and, in retrospect, it would be therapeutic for me as well. This man's name is Art Stanton, and there are many reasons why he is my friend to this day. This declaration of his, this focus, was the impetus for me to write this book. Thank you, Art, for being the guy who kicked our collective butts, implored me to write this book, and for being my friend. I really appreciate it as will the folks who read this book.

Chapter 12

The IEP

IEP: These three letters strike fear into the heart of all involved with disabled children; they stand for Individualized Education Plan. These plans are put into place as a guide for children who are assimilated into mainstream or specialized schools, so that they learn at the pace that is correct for them at the intellectual level they are at currently. The Individuals with Disabilities Education Act (IDEA) says the purpose of an IEP is **"to ensure that all children with disabilities have available to them a free appropriate public education that emphasizes special educa-tion and related services designed to meet their unique needs and prepare them for further education, employment and independent living."** In other words, we must take care of these children so that they can function in society.

When is the IEP developed? An IEP meeting must be held **within 30 calendar days** after it is determined, through a full and individual evaluation, that a child has one of the disabilities listed in IDEA and needs special education and related services. A child's IEP must also be reviewed at least annually thereafter to determine whether the annual goals are being achieved and must be revised as appropriate.

Here's a quick peek of what you could expect from a typical IEP. This document is a working plan pieced together by the school district and the parents of the child for whom it's written. They include but are not limited to the following: What special services are required for your child such as special education classes, OT, PT, etc.; what most communities call SMART goals (specific, measurable, attainable, relevant, timely); where your child fits in from a performance standpoint; how often the reporting will be on your child's goals; some type of document that states where your child will be in the future; and where the least-restrictive place is for your child to learn.

Some items to have at the IEP meeting include, but are not limited to:

1. Pen and paper or an iPad to take down notes.
2. A current copy of the IEP in effect.
3. Any educational evaluations you may have had done on your child.
4. A list of any areas you think your child needs help with.
5. Written questions to ask (you may forget at the meeting), because the meetings tend to get emotional.
6. Some type of folder/binder to keep copies of any document you sign.
7. An open mind...you may not get everything you want, and it's important to have some give-and-take during these discussions.

The special services requirement is just that, to decide what services are needed for your child in a classroom setting that will best allow them to learn. For each child, it will be different as are all unique disabilities. The acronym SMART is a way to scorecard your child against his metrics as defined in the plan.

For instance, if your child has ADHD, what *specific* goal is needed to help him overcome this? It may be something as simple as committing to a single task until he learns it and not overwhelming him with a lesson plan that includes multiple tasks done at one setting. Also these goals have to be measurable (how do we know what success will look like), attainable (not setting too lofty of an expectation on a task), etc. Nothing will set a disabled child back quite like a goal that can never be reached.

Relevancy simply means we don't need to be teaching our children about the dialects of 15th century Mongolia. Let's get their basic building blocks for life started before we get to Genghis Khan. We also have to establish a timeline for these attainable tasks to be done. If the tasks can't be met, the IEP was too aggressive and should be amended. Conversely, if these tasks are quickly mastered, let's also establish new and slightly more difficult examples in an amended IEP.

A disabled child's performance is important when addressing the IEP. You want to neither glorify nor underestimate what your child's true performance really is. You simply want an accurate accounting of what he or she can and cannot do. This isn't to be confused with, "I think he can do that," or "Someday soon he'll get there." Right now, what can your child do? Otherwise you run the risk of an inaccurate build for services for your child. If he needs extra OT, state that.

Do not be afraid to voice your opinion in a professional manner. Once a baseline has been established, services can be allocated on a person-centric basis. In other words, the program won't be built so that your child can fit in; your child's program will be built for their needs to better ensure a successful outcome.

Reporting on an agreed-upon timeline is also worthy of discussion. If your child is severely disabled, maybe a timeline that includes less-frequent reporting may be an agreed-upon goal by all. It may be that one goal is all he can handle, and that's okay, but you may not need such frequent reporting in this example. If your child is slightly disabled and the IEP has multiple goals associated with his success, perhaps a more frequent **reporting of facts** is best. You'd want to know if one or more of his many goals has been attained and to set new goals for him.

What the future holds for your child is dependent on his progress, the expertise of his teachers, OT, PT, and other specialists, and his parents. The IEP usually involves a document that states where your child will be in the future. It's a goal to be worked towards and may or may not be accomplished. No one knows what the future holds, as children can accelerate their learnings, new medicines can help with this, and some-times the disability is degenerative. Use your best estimate of where you realistically hope your child will be next year. If it's at the school he is at currently, state that. If you think he has a decent shot at assimilating into mainstream, state that too. These IEPs are an annual event, and much can change in a single month, never mind a year.

The least-restrictive place for them to learn is code for what gives them the best opportunity to learn. Your local school will tell you they have the qualified help and infrastructure to accomplish this goal. (They may or may not.) I would visit my local school (we did) and ask other parents (we did) who have had or have their children in this setting how the services rate. Do your homework as a caretaker. You are the voice for your child's IEP.

Keep this in mind when at the IEP meeting; it is a collaborative effort between parent and school system, and each municipality is different in its approach. In general, those communities that are better off financially will be more apt to allow a student to attend a specialized school. No budget is limitless, though, and all towns and cities must be accountable to their taxpayers. For residents of less-financially-well-off cities, I would not hesitate to seek counsel if denied a specialized school. I did this, but each person's case is different, and each person should weigh all factors when making this important decision for their child.

If your child attends an agency, rather than your local school system, the next IEP about twelve months later will usually be held at that agency. In attendance will be their teachers (speech, OT, PT), and any other that is mentioned in the original IEP. If the agency has one, and most do, a transition coordinator will also be available if your child is within a couple of years of graduation. A representative from your school district will be in attendance, and a member of the agency itself will be there, usually a director or administrator. All will sign in, and each member reports out in the progress of the student. Those SMART objectives will be addressed by each teacher.

Depending on the progress of the student, a decision will be reached to either keep the student at the agency or assimilate him into the school district. If the progress is less than expected or more is needed for a complete transition to the local school system, the student will usually stay at the agency. Sometimes municipalities have budget cuts, so be prepared to stand your ground.

Have all your documentation ready beforehand and have a meeting with your agency to make sure they have fully documented your child's progress. In our case, we had a professional agency that always had the required docs. I highly recommend starting the process with your agency thirty days before the IEP to ensure all docs that are needed are up to date.

The hope and expectation of every parent is to have their disabled kids progress so much that they can be in a regular school with everyone else. My hope for all of you is that this happens with your child. If that transition is at hand, be one hundred percent sure this is the road you want to travel. The last thing you want for your child is the turbulence in their life that would happen if they aren't ready for that step and they have to go back to the agency.

We have to remember that these are fragile human beings who aren't used to change, and this should carry much weight in your decision making. If they are ready to graduate from that agency into their school system, that means the agency did its job, your child has made massive strides in their education, and life has indeed gotten better for all. A caretaker does what's right for their child.

The first time Laurie and I experienced the IEP was when Derek was about four, and we quickly learned that cost got in the way of making the correct decision. Derek couldn't string two words together, and our town was pushing for him to attend main-stream schools within the special education program. We understood Derek's basic needs, and they understood the cost involved.

We wanted the best option for him to have the best life possible with specialized teachers and programs that would be taught to him by professionals in their field. These schools are readily accessible to the vast majority of Americans. Our town thought they could do the same job at the same level of knowledge and ultimately to the same standards of success.

I immediately sought counsel and paid a handsome amount of money for a lawyer to argue why our son should attend the Sargent Center, our choice. We felt this would give Derek the best possible shot at a fulfilling life, to reach his potential as a person, and we were right.

The difference between the two schools was readily apparent with OT and PT specialists trained to work with disabled children. The level of care was also much better at Sargent; precisely because it cost more, they could care for him, and while our town surely wanted to do a great job, they did not have the same resources available.

Let's talk about costs. Our taxes as members of our town go towards many things: police, fire, ambulance, and of course education. We pay even if we never call the police, never have our house burn down, and never need a ride in an ambulance. We also pay whether or not we have children who go to public school in this town. Our daughter never stepped foot in a public school, which was our choice. We paid for her to go to school here and did not utilize the school system as we sent her to private schools from K-12, again our choice. She never rode on the school bus, never used a town schoolbook, never sat in a classroom in town, yet still we paid our taxes like everybody else.

There are thousands of stories exactly like ours in this town and others across America. My point is that disabled children should be allowed to go to a school that will understandably cost more for the town and its taxpayers to get his best education. We paid taxes for that same education and did not use the service for Haley, and the town saved money from her and hundreds like her.

The towns also receive grant money from the federal government for cases like ours. It covers roughly fifteen percent of the cost of the Sargent Center. If you combine that with the savings of neither of my two children attending public school and hundreds of others, then the net cost is still more expensive but far more reasonable than at first glance. I work hard for my money, and it still bothers me that I had to fight for my child to go a school that was his right to and spend a hefty sum to do so. It bothers me more that it can exclude those who don't have sufficient funds to retain a lawyer, which I find to be beyond unfair.

This isn't a knock on the districts; they are handcuffed by the financial constraints placed upon them by the budget. Education isn't cheap to come by in the first place, and the disabled child does take a disproportionate amount of money as opposed to a regular student. Everyone deserves a good education, and the costs have to be amortized among the student populace. The ratio among disabled children to regular children in the country is about one in seven.

In 2017–18, the number of students ages 3–21 who received **special education services** under the **Individuals** with **Disabilities Education** Act (IDEA) was 7 million, or 14 percent of all **public school** students. Among students receiving **special education services**, 34 percent had specific learning **disabilities**.

If you do some quick math on a graduating class of about 250 students, it's about 35 children who will need special assistance. Of those, maybe a quarter will be enrolled in an alternate school at considerable cost to the district. I could find no data to support this and am relying on my observations at our school district. I'm willing to pay the extra tax every year, so a handful of kids can get the education that is most helpful to them. Another way to look at this is it does minimally help with the reduction in regular school classroom size and is beneficial to both teacher and regular students in this manner.

Stand your ground, come with documentation, and be prepared to hire counsel if you feel you need to for the betterment of your child. If you do these three things, you'll have a much better chance at placing your child in the correct place for him to thrive.

Chapter 13

Derek's Graduation

"Only the day dawns to which we are awake.

Henry David Thoreau

Today is the day! Derek turns twenty-one, and this day brings forth so many emotions. My wife and I have nurtured this child to adulthood, and the journey was filled with heartbreak, joy, trepidation, and higher highs and lower lows than we ever thought possible. From the elation of creating a baby, through the operations, past the IEPs, the trips to what seemed like a thousand doctors, and the incomprehensible thought that today he becomes an adult, we have arrived.

All three of us are here, together, never apart, as it should be. He's a man, capable of freedom according to the government. He is now legal, able to vote, drink, serve his country, drive, and be free from the constraints of those pesky teenage years.

Except Derek has never been a teenager.

Sure chronologically he's been there, but intellectually he will never exist in that space between thirteen and nineteen. And that's okay; it really is. He is forever young, forever a child, and what's not to like about that? How many times do you hear a friend, a sister, a mother utter the words "They grow up so fast!" All the time; that's how many times.

My son will always be my little boy, my main man, my buddy, whatever you would call your child; that's what my child, now twenty-five years old will always be to me. He smiles at cartoons, he laughs at silly jokes, and he still likes to cuddle. At no time will he ever look at me and say the words "I hate you" or roll his eyes at something an uncool parent would do or say. He'll never borrow the car or ask for an extra $20 for a date. You know, those things a teenager would say….

There is a wicked satisfaction in that he will always have that wide-eyed wonderment about him. It's Christmas for him every time we put on his coat, as he knows he's either going outside or for a ride in the car, his absolute favorite thing to do. Most teenagers would rather shoot you through the eyes, burn you at the stake, and maybe even tar-and-feather you than be seen with you (their parents), let alone be in a car with you. Not so for the little man; he will always be happy when I'm giving him his bath, always be happy when Laurie asks him, "Who's the most handsome boy?" and it's in these moments that I fully embrace who I have as a disabled person.

He is never going to be an adult, and he will never be that grownup who will accompany me for a beer and some wings while at a ballgame talking about what the next pitch will be. And that will always be okay with me. Instead, I will enjoy what has been given to me, make the most of the situation all of us are in, and find a workable solution.

I will enjoy my son at his level, whatever that level happens to be. He might be five years old for the rest of his life, he might get to ten, might not. It's up to me to find enjoyment at his intellectual appropriateness and offer guidance and above all acceptance for who he is. I will understand and accept his timeline, because that's what caretakers do.

I'll never be a mother, but I suspect that at the end stages of a mom's life, they harken back to the days when they could hold their child in their arms, pick out their clothes and dress them, reminisce about the teacher-student relationship they enjoyed, and rejoice over the first bicycle ride their children took solo.

It's a long way from where their kids are now, all grown up and with kids of their own, and that life that mom is now replaying in her mind will be filled with those proud moments. I'd like to think that my end stages will be filled with much the same types of thoughts these moms had; I get to experience true love and authentic emotions from a child for decades, not just for a few years. I'm going to take that and run with it for the rest of my years on this planet. These memories are more valuable than gold, and I'm acutely aware of what they mean. I am the luckiest man I know.

We measure our newly born humans through benchmarks of life; he spoke at twenty-one months, he walked at eighteen months, and knew his alphabet at two years old! Freedoms granted to them throughout their lives are important as well. Curfews, sleepovers, phones, dating, cars, jobs, and votes all have a say in regard to maturity, growth, and responsibility. These are all major hurdles with complex thought processes that are taken for granted in a normal life. Our graduates have their own benchmarks to earn, and for special needs parents these are just as satisfying. Maybe even more so, as we have been an integral part of their successes.

You're supposed to drive at sixteen, supposed to vote at eighteen, have a drink at twenty-one. These are recognized accomplishments that all young adults aspire to attain. Sure, sometimes Johnny might lag a bit behind in driving or Sally won't register to vote, but it's the norm in the majority of cases. For our proud graduate, it's more than that. We have seen them accomplish goals that were not even part of the conversation when we first became aware of the initial diagnosis. They have come so far yet still have runway left for more goals to be conquered. We have hope and we are proud!

In the special needs arena, we recognize much smaller goals; Jimmy held a fork today, Susie understood two commands given back to back, Frankie went potty all by himself! There is a huge differentiation in these accomplishments. Neither the normal teenagers nor the special needs child's accomplishments should be considered better. They are just different, that's all.

Laurie and I were just as happy to see our daughter Haley graduate or our son Ryan get married as we are when Derek speaks a new word. The effort expanded by all three to get to that point of accomplishment is equivalent. They have each graduated according to their abilities, and that's what we are here to celebrate.

My non-teenager will never ask for Calvin Klein, Michael Kors, or any other designer for that matter. He doesn't know and doesn't care if he's cool or trendy, hip, or hot. We dress him in sweatpants and loose-fitting clothes that can be easily managed for him and for us. He has a smile on his face when we do so, and for us, the money we save on these designer clothes will be used for his favorite vanilla shake. I'd rather buy a smile than impress others.

He exists as a real person under those no-name clothes, and he's cool with that, as are his parents. There is something truly refreshing about this. It's all the nonsense and the glitter, all the pomp and circumstance, all the elitism of society that is readily not present in this individual that speaks the truth. His veritas is within his heart and soul and within the hearts and souls of his family and friends. What you see with Derek is what you get. It's easy and unassuming, no layers of materialism to sift through, no ulterior motives; it's pure and unadulterated, and it's beautiful to witness.

Today, however, is Derek's special day...he looks fantastic in his navy blue blazer, white button down shirt, khaki pants, Topsiders, and a tie tied by his father. I'm a stickler for a double Windsor to be properly matched to a suit, and today it looks wonderful on this young whippersnapper. He looks like he aged five years from the morning of graduation as his normal garb are those sweatpants and a t-shirt. Realization of his impending graduation is at hand.

He looks manly handsome, all grown up, an adult, and I let myself believe he knows what's going on; it is his day, after all. He has a certain calmness about him, a certain nobility that lets me know he knows something special is going to happen today. I'm okay with being fooled, just for today.

It's a glorious day for November; the sun is shining and it's unseasonably warm. Today is a day that is full of dichotomies, ironies, origins, and endings, and a general sense of melancholy. For fifteen years, Derek was at Sargent Center and for fifteen years my wife dressed and fed him, got him ready for school, loaded him in the car, and made the drive to his school.

She had conversations with the same folks who dropped their kids off to school. She'd dutifully go back in the afternoon to engage in more conversations and pick our boy up. I would get a small taste of her world when I was on vacation, got to know the people she conversed with, but I didn't know them as intimately as Laurie did. I could not imagine what was going through my wife's mind. Today would mark an end to that structured daily routine, and what's next?

We said our greetings to the same people we always did, knowing we would not see them again. Those people at school that we had trusted for all those years would now be removed from his life, and we had no choice in the matter.

And what of Derek? How would he feel, how would he react to a complete restructuring of his day, his life? Would he miss school, his friends, his teachers, his rides in the car? There was so much uncertainty in our immediate future and like most life-changing events, you have to experience it firsthand to find out. You have to take the test to get the answers.

We took the test the next day, and my first inclination was that Derek would be pulling out the school icon from his picture book every hour. Maybe he didn't like school, maybe he would rather stay home with mom, maybe he equated going for a ride in the car with going to school. It was a welcome relief to know he was okay with staying home, and he seemed content with no anxiety whatsoever. It surprised both Laurie and me, but it was a first step towards the unknown and that unknown path would start to get easier to walk as the days flew past.

A big difference in the world of a disabled student is that the federal government graduates you on your twenty-first birthday; everyone graduates alone unless a classmate shares your born day. Special needs indeed; what could be more special than graduating all by yourself, the limelight squarely focused on you and you alone? The place he has called home for fifteen years, the Sargent Center, has baked him a cake, decorated the room with balloons and ribbons, and set up the room with plenty of seating and a podium.

The graduation ceremony starts and the speakers come up and include his case worker from our community, dignitaries from the Sargent Center, his teachers, and finally me. Emotionally I was done before I began to speak. My son, soon to be graduating, looking handsome and dapper, was the culmination of so much work by everyone including those teachers at the Sargent Center who came to see him graduate.

I was keenly aware of what they had done and how they had changed Derek's life and our family's for the better. I needed to thank them and I did in my speech, through my tears and through the conduit of a grateful heart.

Laurie and I had put together a thank-you party the week before for all the teachers and staff at the Sargent Center on behalf of what they had done for our Derek. One teacher in particular struck a chord in my being. She had just lost her husband, but she found the time to write a very poignant card to Derek and us titled "Ten things I like about Derek." Who does this? She had just lost her husband recently and she made sure we knew what Derek had meant to her. I mentioned her and what she had done in my speech. Good deeds should be publicly announced, and I will forever be grateful to her.

The family gets to rejoice too. They have reached a milestone in their world, one where the care and struggle have gotten them this far, to the day they see their child graduate. For me it is most like experiencing a wedding – a time of transition, time to leave your singular past and join with another to fulfill your life's expectation.

This transition for the child/adult sees a slightly different change; they leave their classmates and teachers for a life of two divergent paths. Whether to join a group home or live at home with the help of aides is one of the most difficult decisions special needs parents will ever make, and one where as much information as one can get is the best way to accomplish this.

I'm an emotional man. My heart is on my sleeve for all to observe. On Derek's day of graduation, I was a mess. All the kids were there from the neighborhood. It was an awesome sight for both Laurie and me to see. All of these wonderful young men and women had grown up before our eyes and took the time to attend Derek's graduation.

They had always treated Derek like an equal and always included him in anything they did. It's a special group of young adults I truly believe will be heard from before their purpose in life is over. It's this inclusiveness that had me so emotional; I was a kid who would make fun of kids with disabilities. It's clearly not something I'm proud of and clearly had not forgotten. These kids today were ghosts from my past who allowed me to erase the bad memories and deeds that I had done so many years ago.

In a sense we all graduated with Derek. He taught us all about the best things in life: Never give up, empathize, always keep a smile on your face, and no matter what, just get up every day and do your best. I'd like to think all the Abbotts Crossing kids took something or many things away from their experiences with Derek.

Perhaps he helped them to be a tad more empathetic to their fellow man, to be kind to one another, to be a little unselfish. Perhaps they all realize just how fortunate they are to have their health and welfare and their wits about them. We can all learn something from each other.

My other two children and my wife all graduated as well; each had a difficult road to traverse and a helping hand in bringing Derek to his stage and them to theirs. I graduated too; a more complete human now stands before me in the mirror. I've learned so much along my journey and now experience a wholeness within myself for my family that is at its highest peak. I am proud of my family unit; we've done it, we took Derek to graduation and celebrated him and us on the same day and will continue to celebrate forever.

Chapter 14

Post-Graduation

"Peril, loneliness, an uncertain future, are not oppressive evils, so long as the frame is healthy and the faculties are employed; so long, especially, as Liberty lends us her wings, and Hope guides us by her star."

Charlotte Bronte

Now what? What comes next, what new bridge must we traverse now? Better yet, what bridge must we construct and out of what materials must we make it? The disabled child is now home, and it is a wholesale change for both parents and the child/adult. No more getting ready for school, no more regular *routine,* and that can be a very dangerous situation for all involved. In our case with Derek's autism diagnosis, we had to be aware of any negative behavioral issues stemming from this lack of structure. *Caretakers are behaviorists too.*

Life has been very difficult so far, but we've made it through, and the most important part is our child has journeyed with us. We are here together, one unit, one undefeated unit ready for the next challenge, even those types of challenges we have not seen yet. Together we will win again, just like the thousands of times we've won in the past. The path has not been clean, easy, or obstruction-free, but we have overcome and we will again; our track record tells us that.

Day one. We thought we were prepared, we thought we knew what Derek would do, how he would react, and what our particular game plan would be for that day. We had this one covered. Covered in what I don't know, but we were wrong on most counts. I thought Derek would take a glance at his picture book, pick up the school pic about three dozen times and demand to head out to school. Survey says "uh, no," that's not what happened. If my recollection is on point, he not only did not ask for school at all the first day, it was about thirty days before that pic would be picked up! I'm guessing he didn't enjoy school as much as we thought.

One of the very first learnings for Laurie and me was that his daily class routine may not have been as structured in his mind as much as we had thought it was. Or put a different way, did the Sargent Center do such a good job during his school years that he didn't need this routine that autistic kids hang on to? It's an interesting dichotomy and one that I dwelled on for a bit.

This brings me to a solemn thought: Did he ever miss his friends at school; did he know the feelings of friendship, with all the cliques and quirks? He seemed to enjoy his friends' presence on his good days but with all his seizures, were these thoughts erased from his memory? It's just another in a long line of thoughts and what-ifs that any caring parent would want to know the answers to.

In most disabled children's cases, the communication between parent and child is compromised and frustration can easily set in. Try not to allow these thoughts to muddy your memories and your assumptions about how your child's day went. Latch onto the little smiles, the all-too-fleeting brightening of the eyes, the slight head nods, and other tells that each parent can decipher that lets them know their child has enjoyed at least a part of their day at school. Be happy that the enjoyment they received was good for them, and, by default, good for you and your spouse.

Share these victories, as they are important to everyone. Talk about them at the dinner table, open the conversation with a friend, or if you have joined a support group, chat with people in that group. They are your peers and know what experiences you've gone through better than anyone. Reach out, spill your feelings, and just as important, listen when it's your turn to pay it back.

How about his teachers and the aides, or the parents he would see at start and end of the school day? Does he have a memory of all this? It's a fair question, one for which I will never receive an answer, but it intrigues me nonetheless. However, I have learned, and I will not dwell on this, as it steals from my happiness and the happiness of my child. Each day is a new beginning and with it brings new challenges that we must overcome.

As they say, there is nothing quite so shallow as yesterday's applause. Each day we have to earn our keep, and these questions, these what-ifs, must be kept in check; otherwise, the day, as hard as it's going to be naturally, may become a bit more difficult. Look for the good in everything. Stay positive.

Post-graduation is also a time of change for the parents, who now must become full-time caretakers for their child. Another option is a group home. Neither is automatically correct for any given situation, as all cases are uniquely different. For the most part, states are getting away from managing day-to-day care for disabled adults. There are many reasons for this: skyrocketing costs, the ever-present threat of lawsuits, real estate prices, community NIMBY movements, etc. What matters is that you do your research and pick the right fit for your unique situation.

There are many moving parts, including transportation, medical and prescription duties, and a real shortage of skilled workers because of an abysmal pay rate. Oddly, the closing or scaling back of some of these homes will put more caretakers on the market to choose from. Add all of these factors in, and the obvious move towards home placement is and probably will be taking place at an accelerated pace.

The first path takes the shape of matching five or more adults, so that their strengths complement each other; one might be functional at cooking, and one might enjoy cleaning, so that the totality of the household is capable of living together successfully with the help of an aide. This is also a very expensive way of housing and assimilating these adults into society. The latest estimate from my home state is $100,000 per annum for each disabled child.

The aides who care for these adults are often extremely underpaid, and it is not an occupation college graduates flock to. Also, state funds and federal funds are not bottomless, and this method is simply not sustainable for all disabled kids who enter adulthood.

The second method, which is gaining traction and becoming more mainstream with more recent graduates, ensures the child stays with his parents at home, as this is most always the less-expensive option. It varies from state to state, but the child is assigned a level of need and the family is given a number of hours that may be used for care to come into the household. There is no single correct answer for each family/child. The decision is based on many factors; work, health of the parents as well as the child, finances, etc.

We chose to keep Derek at home. For us, the decision was an easy one. He has many seizures on any given day, and they are potentially dangerous to his health, given the fall risk. He takes medicine five times a day, and who would administer that in a group home setting? The hours we were given are put to good use. We have multiple caregivers who give Derek direction and teach him in different ways. This also allows Ms. Laurie the chance to leave her domicile, to get out into the real world, to shop, to grab a cup of coffee, to see other *adults*.

It's just as important for her mental health to get out into society and breathe, get her groove on, let Laurie be Laurie. It doesn't take much for her to be happy, and she deserves a "time-out" as much as anyone. *Caretakers need to be freed from their shackles too.*

Pre-graduation, a parent will sit with the outplacement service at the school their child attends and study the options available to them. A child will be graded on a sliding scale much like a report card, with A being the least needy and therefore least funded, down through the alphabet until you reach the medical designation. The funding is commensurate with the grading, meaning that you will receive funds to be used at your discretion for home OT, PT, or speech, usually utilizing skilled professionals to aid in your now adult's continued growth.

A caution to the parent on this meeting where your child is to be graded: Stay professional and try to take the emotion out of your argument. The final grade can be a blow to who you think your child is and how he is ultimately graded. It can be hard to understand the grading concepts and how they arrived at their decision. "My child is better than that," or "My child can't be scored this high or low" are two of the common opinions of parents at this initial meeting.

It is extremely important that you fight for the correct grade for your child/adult. This SIS score (Supports Intensity Scale) will determine the amount of money available for you to use to help your now disabled adult. You obviously want the correct grade and therefore the most money to facilitate growth in your disabled adult.

Here's how it initially works: A dollar amount is assigned based on the grade given to your adult. With these dollars in mind, you can now decide how they shall be spent. Think of it as a bank account that has value for your disabled adult. How best can you spend this money to add value to your disabled adult? How can you make their quality of life the best it can be given your options? The answers are different for everyone as the disparity in disabilities is enormous. For some folks, it may be constant care if the level of disability is high, and for some, it may hinge on getting the adult out into society so they can assimilate in public or become employed.

In the first example, more money would be in your bank account given the high level of disability and also the higher cost of care. It makes sense that an RN would cost more per hour than a CNA, and that adds a level of complexity to your decisions. In this case, say you receive $70,000 from your state agency per year. The question now becomes: How many hours do you need to provide maximum value for your child/adult?

The salary difference between an RN and a CNA is about $30,000 per year in my neck of the woods. It's true you get what you pay for, so use those funds wisely. You'll have about $1,400 weekly to spend, and the $30,000 difference is about $600 weekly or $15 an hour! You will run out of hours at nearly twice the pace of an RN vs. a CNA. It's neither good nor bad, just a metric you need to consider for the best *value* for your situation. My reasoning would be that the higher level of care needed, the more you would allocate those dollars towards specified care to ensure the best value.

One other note on this with respect to finding the right qualified person. In many areas of the country, there is a shortage of persons available for these roles. If you get lucky and find a person who is qualified, who is a great fit for your adult, and who offers consideration for your child, keep them around at all costs.

You and only you determine the pay rate for your adult's care. It makes great sense to overpay someone to keep them, foster good will, and enable your adult the opportunity to grow through their qualified care. The flip side is that you choose to pay market value or worse underpay, and you'll then become an expert at interviewing people and watching soaps.

Once qualified help finds out about the subpar hourly rate, you won't see or hear from them after the interview; you will have a revolving door at your house with very little chance to employ these folks. Once word gets out that you don't pay, you won't even get to interview folks as they won't come at all and you can watch *All My Children* instead of having the assistance you need. Do not be that caretaker who doesn't see the forest for the trees!

The adult who is less challenged with their particular disability may not need as much skilled supervision as a child who may have limited mobility. This is a decision that must not be taken lightly. There has to be a balance between OT, PT, socialization, and addressing the particular needs of each adult. It's a whole new ballgame, and one where you have to prioritize your adult's needs by what you would like to see them accomplish.

In their child life, the school or agency mostly did this work for you. Now that the adult phase of their life is here, you need to be cognizant of their needs and wants from a learning perspective. Again, the right mix of the above categories is unique to each adult and parent. Maybe your household doesn't have a car during the day as one spouse is using it for work, so it could be a perfect time to have an aide come in and take your adult to the movies, out to eat, visit a park, or a bowling alley; the possibilities are indeed endless.

Perhaps your adult wasn't getting the best OT from his agency, so if you see the potential for significant improvement, by all means tailor the program for more hours of OT than socialization. Most of these adults with disabilities will live a very fluid life with multiple ebbs and flows in their learning programs. It's up to us as parents to advocate the best program available at the time they need it.

What looks good one month may not be the best program the next month. Know your disabled adult's limitations and get them there; if that limit can be topped, ensure that the program gets more difficult but attainable. There may not be a greater joy on earth than witnessing a disabled adult accomplish something special. I don't care if it's saying the alphabet, going potty by herself, or saying a word never before said; the feeling is special for both parent and the disabled adult. *Remember to celebrate.*

Stay in touch with other families in the same or similar situation you are in. The world of disability from an operational standpoint is ever-changing. New laws are being written, new funding becomes available, and benefits that once excluded participants may now include them. You would not want to miss out on any potential benefits for your adult because you weren't up to speed.

This is another new hat you must wear and job you must become proficient at if you want the best possible life for your adult. I implore you to join support groups and learn as much as you can through the internet. Let Google be your friend, and interact with others on what has worked best for them and just as important, what hasn't.

Depending on the level of disability, you may want to check out specific websites for your adult's most compelling issue. In our case, Derek has a form of epilepsy called Lennox-Gastaut, and it's rare. You'll find a wealth of information on any epilepsy website, which is informative and very helpful; however, if you really want to succeed in the search for particular information, you must research the particular issue.

Don't get hung up on information that is general in nature to the issue at hand; get granular and specific as quickly as you can so that you can be in lockstep with any health official you may encounter. The better you can understand the specific issue, the better your results will be in finding a potential cure, appropriate medication, or innovative solutions. Work with the doctors by being informed and knowledgeable. *Caretakers do research.*

All of this brings us back to a central theme: Be flexible, look out to a certain time horizon but understand that the daily routine can be changed on a dime. It's okay, it really is; this is your new normal. Embrace this as yours because it is. It's not your neighbor's, it's not your sister's or your uncle's; it's yours. Own it, be proud of it, and accept it for what it is. That old axiom, comparison is the thief of joy, will marinate in your mind and we don't want that. We want what is the best for your now adult disabled person.

The new beginning is here and you'll get used to it, just like you have for their first twenty-one years. You're still here, your child/adult is still here, and you must have succeeded all this time or you wouldn't be reading these words. You can do it, you will do it, and you are not alone. That empathy we talked about for others will always be by your side, and I cannot think of a better voice than the one that says you are fighting for your own flesh and blood.

Chapter 15

Group Home vs. Home-Based Care

After a disabled child turns twenty-one, caretakers have another difficult decision to mull over. In the eyes of the government, that child is now a disabled adult, and the transition from child to adult is never easy. Add in all the complexities of a disabled adult, and the process can be a formidable experience. All the services they used to receive as a disabled child at the facility they just graduated from will now be given at one of two places: a group home or in your own residence as part of a home-based therapy. This will be a difficult process to first understand and then once understood, to make the call on where the best place to be is for your now adult disabled person.

The lack of qualified healthcare professionals is a widespread problem in this country, and for disabled adults it's no different. The pay is low, the conditions are less than stellar, and the job requires a tremendous amount of knowledge. This knowledge comes at a cost of expensive college tuition and is why the shortage is so acute. It's like having that bad day on the golf course; you mean I paid to humiliate myself on this course? Healthcare workers will tell you they do indeed feel humiliated often, and it does take a special person to do what they do every day. In a group home setting, the shortage is the same as home-based, but they can allocate resources as needed. Someone will fill in a shift here or take on responsibility at a different house to get care, with reduced frequencies in some cases, but care nonetheless.

In home-based therapy, the caretaker is responsible for inter-viewing and hiring any OT/PT professionals they can find. It can be incredibly challenging to locate these people in the current economic climate as they can work elsewhere for much better pay. This information given is designed to help you make a choice; my hope is that you will find it to be helpful.

SIS measures the individual's support needs in personal, work-related, and social activities in order to identify and describe the types and intensity of the supports an individual requires. SIS was designed to be part of person-centered planning processes that help all individuals identify their unique preferences, skills, and life goals.

The supports approach also recognizes that individual needs change over time, and that supports must change as well. They must be developed and delivered in age-appropriate settings, with the understanding that, regardless of intellectual abilities or limitations, people should have the opportunity engage in activities and life experiences just like any other person.

The grading will be from A to E and is just like a detailed report card, showing what strengths and weaknesses or opportunities your adult possesses. The grade of A provides the least amount of funding and means your adult is in the least disabled cate-gory. The D and E designations means your adult needs the most care and therefore provide the most funding. I stress once more how important it is at these transitional meetings to get the correct grade as the funding that is received is tied directly into the grade given.

It could mean the difference between enrolling in a program your disabled adult really needs and going without that program altogether. It is far easier to debate the grade given while in these transition meetings than it is to change that grade afterwards. Do your homework and be prepared!

The second step is to assess who you are, honestly and without prejudice. What exactly is your current situation regarding the following areas: health, employment, geographic stability, dependence on relatives for assistance, difficulty of care for your adult, your temperament, and social expectations? This will go a long way towards determining where to place your adult. This assessment should not be taken lightly; if the snapshot of who you are is materially inaccurate, your ultimate decision on where to place your adult will probably be inaccurate as well.

Most folks tend to exaggerate how healthy they are and over-estimate how much help they will receive from their relatives and friends. Do not fall into this trap. Here's the fallout: "My knee hurts a little. Aunt Betty can clear some time on her schedule to help." Ask how much better that knee will feel when tending to your adult and good ol' Aunt Betty has better things to do than clearing her schedule. A more likely scenario is that she'll be sending you a postcard on her cruise to the hospital where you are recovering from knee surgery!

How is your health with regard to cardio? How are you in shape physiologically? If you are marginal and in decline with a possible disability yourself, you may want to add an emphasis on PT help if your desire is to be home-based. Disability includes a history of smoking, COPD, carpal tunnel, or any family history that would indicate a downturn after a certain age. Here's why. The older the caretaker gets, the less muscle mass and less available cardio one has access to. It's straight physiology;

testosterone declines and it becomes harder to maintain either function. You can help yourself by having a program at home for yourself or a gym membership.

The flip side is this. Your adult probably isn't going to lose weight and, in fact, will probably gain. If your health is deteriorating and the physical load you are required to care for is accelerating, what do you think the end result will be? That's right; you or your disabled adult will be harder to handle and you or your adult will get hurt. And where does that leave you? Up that creek without a paddle, that's where. It can be the difference between placing your adult in a group home and keeping him with you. *Caretakers stay fit.*

What does your employment look like from a caretaker perspective? Have you been at your job for a while? Is your job stable? If you lost your job, would it cause undue financial stress on your household? All of these have important considerations when making your decision. Remember, your disabled adult has a fixed income, and it's a supplement, not meant to provide for anything more than a basic, meager existence.

You are responsible for him financially. In most households, if there is a major breadwinner, the household can easily support a disabled adult as the adult really doesn't cost that much extra to live there. Sure, they'll use a marginal amount extra of utilities and, of course, the extra food; however, that's where the SSI or SSDI check is helpful. Ask yourself if the household could run on your unemployment check and their disability check. Do you have a nest egg available for times exactly like this? There is much to think about and discuss ahead of your decision.

Where are you domiciled as a caretaker? Is the home a safe haven for your adult? Would a move to a new home or a group home adversely affect your disabled adult? In our case, with Derek's autism diagnosis, there is a strong possibility the move could have less-than-desirable results for all. Do you as the caretaker have a desire to move to a warmer climate when you retire? Is the move in response to a health condition that could be alleviated by a warmer, drier climate? If so, congratulations; you have an unenviable set of circumstances to try and figure out.

So what happens in a case like this where there are mitigating circumstances? The welfare of your adult disabled person should always prevail. If the move to a new address will be so upsetting to his emotional balance, then a placement in a local group home may be an option you could discuss with your support group. Another difficult decision to think about...

What is the level of difficulty care-wise for your adult? There are many dimensions to discuss: medicine administration, hygiene including bathing and toiletries, dressing, feeding. Is your adult ambulatory? How is their temperament? All of these need to be considered when making your decision. Honesty is the best policy, so reach out to any friends you have who can be object-ive when discussing your adult. Your expertise at guiding your child/adult through all of these processes has been honed for years, sometimes decades. You may think it's just a walk in the park to care for your disabled adult because you're so good at it. But enlist your friends to give their feedback.

Look from someone else's perspective as to the complexity of the services you provide. I'm pretty sure not too many people would enjoy wiping a butt or cleaning up puke. How many medicines and how many doses does your adult need daily? What are the ramifications of missing a dose? Before you pull the trigger on home care, be aware of the dangers and side effects of missing med time. You may want to leave it in the hands of a professional in a group home setting. If you have competent help coming in and can adjust those meds to a different timeline that helps to eliminate missed meds time, then maybe your home is best.

How is your temperament? Is it up to the challenge of taking care of another person essentially fulltime? This is where you have to be totally honest with yourself yet again. Ask others for their opinion of you, but don't ask anyone you know who will sugarcoat it as this will just make it worse in the short term. If your own personality is one that gets frustrated or angered easily, I would think that you either seek medication or therapy (maybe both) to be able to cope with the incredibly stressful life you are about to enter.

If you don't want to do either or feel like they wouldn't work for you, I strongly suggest you take a look at a group home for your adult. If you already have multiple stressors in your life such as other children, a high-stress job, parents who are not in good health, geographically distant relatives, either acknowledge that this will be a tough road and handle it like a rock star or think about a group home setting. This will be the hardest job you've ever had and the most rewarding as well. It does, however, come with difficult options that must be weighed beforehand.

Social expectations are something to think about when caring for a disabled adult. Are you the type that has to go see a movie every week, visit a long-lost friend, likes to go out to eat, or enjoys hobbies that require a lot of time like golf, for instance?

In a word, sacrifices must be made in the world of disability, and if you're not willing to curtail or cut back altogether some of the activities mentioned here, you may not be a candidate as a home-based caretaker. Let's face it: As caretakers of adults, we are probably approaching fifty years old or older and are dreaming of the days where all the hard work we've done can now start to be enjoyed as we hope to relish our favorite hobbies. Try to tailor those hobbies or modify them, so your adult can either join in or safely watch from the sidelines.

It's okay to be social, but the days of playing eighteen holes on a Saturday are probably not going to happen. You can be flexible and play nine on a Tuesday; just recognize that the social life you led before may be compromised more than you thought. This is the sacrifice that must happen if your adult is to be in home-based care. If you are not willing to compromise to this new standard, do your adult and yourself a favor and think strongly about a group home environment. The animosity you hold towards your child will emotionally damage both of you and is not a healthy environment for either.

Here's something else to think about. I have a friend I've known since high school who has a disabled daughter. Her story is a difficult one in that she became a single parent by divorce although the father was completely in the picture and by her account was a fantastic dad. When her daughter was sixteen, the unthinkable happened; her ex-spouse died, and she was left alone to care for her daughter.

Since she still needed to be employed, she designed a solution by placing her daughter in a group home setting during the week and picked her up every weekend. My friend found herself in one of the worst positions in her life, in my opinion, yet still was able to be flexible, compromise, and make it work for all. It's just an example of a great solution that works for her and her daughter, and I commend her for her bravery and stoicism. There are options available, and the caretaker has to be creative to find the best answer in their particular situation.

Assistance by relatives or friends is an absolute luxury in the caretaker's world and should be seen as such. This is what I like to call the X factor. If they are truly available to help out, then any of the categories that we've spoken about here can be remedied. If you have health issues, if your employment is at risk, or if you find yourself temporarily out of a job, this X factor will really come in handy. If Uncle Frank is nearby, perhaps he could assist with watching your adult for a bit while you go food shopping. It might be you need a ride to the mechanic's to get your car back after being serviced, or you might need help for a half hour or so with showering your adult. You get the picture.

Another fantastic positive from having local relatives or friends is the social bonds they provide. I'm quite sure this cannot be overemphasized; the social interaction for the disabled adult and the caretaker may be of equal value. Sometimes it's just good to see another soul during the day to break the monotony and help with maintaining a positive outlook on your life.

There are many moving parts to our lives of disability management; research and understand each in a comprehensive document to yourself that outlines the good, the bad, and the ugly. Gathering of all pertinent information is critical to making any decision, let alone one that will affect the well-being of your adult disabled person. My motto is always to simplify any decision big or small: Draw a simple T graph with advantages on the left and disadvantages on the right. In descending order of importance, place any advantage you may think of on the left and compare it with the disadvantage on the right.

You may find that certain issues cancel each other out. What you originally thought of as the number one issue may in fact be down the list a bit. It's a working document; concentrate on getting as much real info on there as possible. Once it's completed, take a hard look to determine if you are convinced that the order of importance is correct. Give extra weight to those issues at the top and less to those at the bottom. Set these priorities and make a decision based on facts, not conjecture.

Another consideration is your age as a caretaker and the age/condition of your spouse, if you have one. I can't tell you firsthand how the sixties feel, but I'm almost there at fifty-eight years old. Up until my very early forties, I was Superman. I had the S emblazoned on my chest; I'd show it to you but it fell off. There is a large difference in physical capability now versus then. I'm quite sure this chasm will only grow as I age into my seventies. It's why I do my best to stay in good physical form.

Most folks reading this will be in their early to mid-forties when their child graduates on their twenty-first birthday. Physically you're starting to feel the decline, but your financial ability to take care of your now adult starts to improve as you age. Pensions, IRAs, and 401ks all generally improve with longevity, and your debt is paid down year after year. The day of reckoning will come, though, when you are no longer able to take care of your adult. It's a bit of a paradox: As you start to fail physically, your financial picture improves so you could bring in extra help, being careful not to outlive your savings. It's not easy making these decisions; however, preparation beats inaction every time.

You must be aware of this financial conundrum, as it could be disastrous for all. Nobody will be better off if the funds run dry. Flexibility; there's that word again. The time to place your child in a group home setting will come and it's not the end of the world. You'll be able to visit and bring him home for the weekends while being cognizant of the financial shortfall you would have been facing had this move not been made. Stay away from feelings of guilt at this stage of your lives. You've sacrificed so much for your child/adult, and you cannot end up on the street with no place to live. It's called being responsible for all and being unselfish. *Caretakers constantly re-evaluate.*

The final decision is yours as a caretaker. It should be given great thought and insight for what is best for your child/adult.

Chapter 16

Adults Who Become Disabled

A different type of disability/caretaker relationship we haven't talked about is one involving adults who have become disabled much later in life. These people deserve a seat at this table too. The dynamic is often much different, as after sixty or more years of knowing this person, often a parent, as a normal, able-bodied adult, they have now become forgetful, incontinent, non-ambulatory, or fragile physically. It's a lot to handle, and in some respects, it's a more difficult transition. They can't get sick; it's mom or dad, for crying' out loud! Dad built our house, and mom raised the four of us while holding down a full-time job.

The top diseases for these symptoms of late life disability are Alzheimer's and Parkinson's. There are, of course, other types of disability such as COPD and heart disease, but for the most part, these diseases can be managed with moderate effectiveness, medicine, and a health regimen. Not so with these two diseases, though, as once diagnosed they are unfortunately a death sentence. Parkinson's is documented as a ten- to twenty-year expected living period, while Alzheimer's is around three to eleven years. Currently five million people have Alzheimer's in the USA, while Parkinson's affects one million. America is growing old rapidly, and these numbers are expected to grow significantly.

By 2050, it is projected that AD will account for fourteen million cases in the USA; right now, it is the sixth leading cause of death. One in ten people age sixty-five and over is currently living with AD and two-thirds of the patients are women. Here's a statistic to consider; 10,000 Americans celebrate their sixty-fifth birthday daily! AD strikes twice as hard in the African-American community, and one and a half times as hard in the Hispanic community.

The methodology behind this rise in AD is ironic. The relative increase of cures, medicines, and therapies for major contributors of death means that people who would have died from say, heart disease, are now living long enough to experience AD. The life expectancy has risen for all because of the reduction in other major diseases, such as cancer, and this has a dual effect on the caretaker. They are now living longer and the likelihood of them caring for someone with AD increases as well. You now have the unenviable situation of an older caretaker caring for an even older AD patient, who is about as high maintenance as you get in the disability universe.

The AD caretaker demographic looks like this: One in three is over sixty-five, two in three are women, and incredibly one in three is the daughter of these patients. One in four caretakers is in what they call the sandwich generation; they care for not only a dementia patient but also have someone in their household under eighteen that they care for.

Twice as many AD caretakers experience substantial emotional, financial, and physical hardships than caretakers of other disabilities. This is precisely why I dedicated a chapter to AD in this book. All the advice I've given to other disabilities such as joining support groups or visiting a therapist and practicing self-care take on an enhanced perspective with this awful disease. In these days of social media, there are many groups you can join online that will validate your feelings and really help you through your caretaking days. Don't be too proud to use any of these platforms, or you'll be the one losing out and by default so will your patient.

Recall that my mother suffered from early-onset AD, and my own experience validates these findings. It's a different subset of disability with more depression and frustration on the caretaker's mindset. The AD patients have demonstrated the ability to do many of the tasks proficiently that they now can no longer finish, and that is at the heart of the frustration.

Many caretakers have witnessed first-hand growing up with mom and dad and what they can do; they have been taught by these very same people how to do those tasks. To watch someone fail at an ordinary task or not to remember what you literally just told them about ten seconds ago is hard to watch.

It's the reverse of what most disabilities are all about. Instead of trying to enable your disabled person to get better, your disabled adult must now be managed to try to not get worse. They aren't going to get better, and this is a bitter pill to swallow. We as caretakers must accept this and manage it in a graceful way. Most times we see progress in our disabled children; it may be small and insignificant in the big picture, but hope is always there for a better outcome. With AD, the best days and progress are always in the past, and it gets worse as the disease continues. The caretaker needs an extra layer of Superman to get through these days. So wash those capes and put on that uniform; you can do it!

For this purpose, we will focus on traditional AD and not early-onset Alzheimer's, which, as the name dictates, affects folks as early as their forties and is mostly driven by genetics. Parkinson's may be even harder to deal with, as physical deterioration is evident with tremors, stiffening of muscles, fatigue, and poor balance. Additionally, speech is impacted both in volume and in forming words. Communication can be difficult at best, which only adds to the anxiety level felt by both patient and caretaker.

For Alzheimer's, the extra focus is not only on safety for the person with the disease, but for the entire household. Here's why. The forgetfulness is the driving force behind many of the safety issues. If dad leaves on the back burner on the stove, if he leaves the bathtub water running, if mom walks outside in Montana in January without her coat or drives somewhere and doesn't remember how to get back, less-than-desirable outcomes will happen.

The first two examples are obvious safety issues for the household, as the house could burn down or suffer serious damage if not caught in time. Getting lost has its own set of problems, as mom may need other medications that support good health and must be taken. Additionally, many other folks are put at risk trying to locate her.

Unlike most disabled adults, our friends who suffer from AD and PD have a date with death that is much more predictable. This creates anxiety for the caretaker mostly rather than the patient. However, it also provides for a great deal of planning that can be more precise for end-of-life events. With these two types of disabilities, nursing home care or assisted living is a near certainty.

We all start out with great resolve to do our duty and take care of our elderly patients, but the level of care needed is extra-ordinary and will tax the best of us to provide top tier care for our loved ones. There comes a point in all of our lives where we must recognize how the whole situation is impacting us. Our jobs, our family, our social lives, and our disabled parent's needs all must be balanced honestly, and it's not an easy conversation. At some point, and it's different for all, the decision must be made that the care you give is substandard to the care they could receive in a professional facility.

Self-care. Let's get back to that for a minute. One of my friends is caring for an AD patient at home. It's very stressful; she knows it's stressful but continues to fight the good fight. My friend visited an optometrist for a routine exam and found out she had broken blood vessels in her eyes. What's the issue, you may ask? This is a clear sign of extremely high blood pressure. She has her BP checked and sure enough, it's off the charts. She is now on medication. *When the love of self is compromised for the love of another,* it's time to take a look at professional care.

Family squabbles. We all have them, and we deal with them in our own ways. If your family history of disagreements starts to get worse, some serious sniping starts to occur, and you can't sit down and talk about it civilly, you may be seeing the initial signs that it's time for professional care. Do not minimize the help you may need, as the life you lead is exceptionally difficult.

Your AD or Parkinson's patient is a traumatic mental health load for the entire family and coupled with the hopelessness of recovery is a bad recipe for good mental health for the care-taker. This mental health affects everyone in the family and when this occurs, major issues are at the doorstep. My go-to person in my time of need is my wife; before I met her, it was my mother. And if I can't talk to my wife, it's my brother. Family is the blanket of reason, of comfort, of solidarity, and if you don't have a healthy coping mechanism that you can go to, it spells doom for the success of all in the family.

Some helpful tips from the Mayo Clinic on caretaking for Alzheimer's patients include keeping a routine, scheduling efficiently, removing safety concerns, eliminating distractions, and including choices that involve the person. It's probably safe to say that most people do their best work when rested.

Try to take that same outlook when approaching your AD patient. Let them wake up, eat breakfast, acclimate to their surroundings, and have them tackle the tasks you've laid out for the day. It could be coloring, picking out an outfit, or choosing what they want to eat for breakfast. Include them by giving a choice of coloring books, breakfast items, or what they may want to wear for the day. Let them keep what dignity they have left by allowing them a choice in their day.

Safety can be enhanced by providing cameras, and locking doorways, drawers, stairwells, and chemical storage areas, such as under the sink. Declutter, get rid of those tripping hazards, and avoid any extensions cords or tape them down if you must. Take a look at your water heater thermometer setting. If it's too high, consider lowering it to prevent burns. Take a walk in their shoes, and you'll uncover potential hazards in your home. Your job as a caretaker is to provide a safe environment; consider these tips as a starting point.

Financially, AD can pose some unique challenges as the specialized care required for this type of disability often comes at a much higher cost than in traditional nursing home situations. The average cost across the country is approximately an additional $1,000 per month. This equates to $12,000 per year or about two extra months' payments per year for a traditional nursing home. I structured the math this way so you could see the impact AD had on finances. If an AD patient were to stay at a specialized Alzheimer's nursing home for four years, it would be the same cost as if they stayed at a traditional nursing home for four years and eight months.

This is something to consider if AD runs in your family, as moving any assets out of the patient's name becomes even more time-sensitive. At an average cost of $4,000 vs. $5,000 monthly, the assets of the patient run out that much quicker. It's hard to believe but the math doesn't lie; four years @ $48,000 equals $192,000, and four years at $60,000 equals $240,000, or nearly a quarter-million dollars!

The money goes quickly, and as a caretaker you must protect the money as soon as possible. Once more, this is even more difficult with an AD patient as loss of mental faculties can inhibit correct decision making well before the onset of recognizable symptoms. Money can be spent innocently by making multiple house payments or credit card bills as they truly forgot when they last paid them. It's no secret people will prey on these types of folks, and they may be duped into buying a timeshare on the beach in Kansas among other scams.

In almost all cases the cared-for AD patient is a family member of more affluent financial means, and this should serve as a reminder to protect that inheritance at all costs while providing safety and care for your loved one. If you have a family with multiple responsible adults, you can distribute the powers of attorney to reduce the stress level for all. If all members are comfortable appointing one POA as a point person while collaborating behind the scenes, that's certainly another option.

If you see mom or dad faltering a bit with memory loss, it could be a thousand things; your job is to not dismiss it as trivial. Recall my story about my mother at Christmas and be a better detective than I was. Not saying the outcome would have been different, but the financial impact could have been. Since my mother's death in 2004, Medicaid has increased the lookback period in nursing homes from two to five years. *Time does matter.*

Chapter 17

Who Will Take Care of Your Child/Adult When You Are No Longer Alive?

"If you would not be forgotten as soon as you are dead, either write something worth reading or do something worth writing."

Benjamin Franklin

This will be the hardest chapter both to read and comprehend, because no one in our disabled fraternity, and I mean no one, wants to go there. Who allows themselves the honesty to think about their own death, but also their disabled child's? It's not a thought that on a given day you'd give credence to, not something that comes up in normal conversation.

There are two reasons for that, neither good: "I don't want to cross that bridge," or "I haven't really thought about it." Let me be the first to admonish you for both non-thoughts. If you have thought about it and aren't acting on it, shame on you. If you haven't thought about it, shame on you. _But you have to prepare for both_....

We all know death is a certainty. As with seemingly every other issue we deal with, it's more complicated with a disabled adult. This is just another problem we have to solve for. A word of caution here; it will possibly be the hardest problem to solve. Ignoring it doesn't make it go away. If you don't think about it, you risk the health and welfare of your child and the forfeiture of assets you have accumulated in life. Remember the mountain-type problems we've all encountered? Yeah, this is the Everest of them of all. But we can do it, we've solved major issues before, we're still here, and we're going to do it again. *Caretakers never give up.*

Your life and that of your child/adult has been fraught with one issue after another. You've been faced with many life-altering decisions, and sometimes they contradict each other. Sometimes the choices are between bad and worse. Every day it can seem like there is a conspiracy out there in Karma land that simply says, "You ain't having a good day today, girlfriend." But every night we get to sleep, and every morning we get to wake with a fresh start and we grind on, we persevere, we get it done.

Every decision you have made in the past has built your suit of armor, has reinforced your shield, and has sharpened your blade. You are ready for any decisions that come your way, and you should be proud of yourself for all you've accomplished. You're ready to make any decision, even this one, because of the success you've crafted for yourself and your child/adult. Do not let this decision distract you from what are most important; the welfare and safety of your adult.

Climbing our mountain is a continual learning process; the landscape is always changing and the issues we solve for prepare us for the next one, like a stepping stone in a pond. Look at this complex issue as the capstone to solve for. I can tell you, my wife will not talk about the day Derek may no longer be here. It bothers her that much, and I respect that and do not bring up the conversation about Derek one day dying.

There are some sobering statistics about the life expectancy of a disabled child; however, you may outlive your children and the thought of this will break many hearts. There have been multiple studies done, and with the wide range of disabilities involved, it's easy to understand that the more severe the physical disability, the shorter the projected lifespan. The possibility exists of your disabled adult perishing before you do, and if you are aware, you ought to be preparing for this worst-case scenario. It's not easy to read about, not easy to talk about, but it must be addressed by the caretaker.

Recent studies, however, have shown that the gap is closing from decades ago about the lifespans of disabled adults. This is great news and is attributable to the many advances in medicine and operational procedures. One of the many challenges involved in medicines and operations is the relative lack of communication available from the disabled patient to the medical professional. Most information will come from the caretaker with little to no help from the patient.

Note-taking is of great importance to protect your child from any side effects from medicines and new therapies. Get yourself some type of manuscript. It can be a three-part notebook like we have, a Word document, or pieces of loose leaf paper held together by a folder. *Start one*.

We like to call ours Derek's Bible; we write down any info we may have gotten from any doctor, therapist, support groups, or any research we may have done on our own. We have been told by nearly all of Derek's doctors that we are the most prepared caretakers they have in their client base. I am extremely proud that my wife has been so diligent about it. Laurie has been an outstanding recorder and the guardian of this legacy information. It is something we can go back over, twenty years in some cases, and see who Derek visited, what medicines worked and what did not.

Many medicines change formulas all the time, and new medicines become available seemingly every month. Patents run out, and a generic version becomes available. Medicines for the most part belong to families, and it may be that something in the formula that has changed or the fundamentals of the medicine and its delivery agent have changed. Keeping good notes is another job the caretaker must be willing to do for their child.

How many people reading this book have great friends? Nearly everyone will say, sure! I have tons of great friends. Sure you do. Ask your so-called best friend this question; "Dear Mrs. Friend, the one I've known for twenty-five years and would trust with my life: *Will you take care of my disabled child when I die?*"

Now, go out and ask any one of your tons of great friends that question. Better yet, see if you can identify even one who would carry that burden for you. How about this from a different angle: Would you even *ask* your best friends that question, knowing how difficult that road would be for them? It is such an enigma, such a difficult situation that has no definite answer, certainly no absolute correct answer.

Here are some guidelines that may help. Start with your family and ask the mentally challenging and important questions inside your own consciousness that will satisfy you beyond any doubt. Be fair and non-judgmental. Don't assume anything about any one of your family members. Will Uncle Johnny be able to care for our now-adult disabled person? One who now weighs 175 lbs., who is adult size and capable of physically hurting anyone, as he doesn't know his own strength, and who may not have the capacity for empathy? Ask who is capable to administer medication, and who is able to pick those medicines up from the pharmacy. Ask who can take him to the doctor's, who can renew all his licenses, and medical and marijuana dispensary cards. This is a real-life troublesome thought and one that plays out across the world of disability every week.

Here are some real-life examples. A mother is found in a bloody mess on her kitchen floor because her son decided to beat her up or grabbed a knife and stabbed her. Consequently, a father has to make the unenviable decision to place his son in a mental institution because of what just happened. Another example is Jane went missing, and a caretaker says, "I have no idea how this happened or where she might be." I know, let's just call her, she'll pick up and we'll go get her...we all know it doesn't work that way with a disabled person. There is no cell phone to reach them on, and they may not have the capacity for even rudimentary communication. This is just another example of the unique situations we face as caretakers, trying to find a non-caretaker who understands these situations like we do.

These are awful, horrible stories that make the headlines in your local newspapers or on the internet. In the example above, a father has to balance the safety of his wife versus that of his son. These are gut-wrenching types of choices that people who love their disabled child have to make nearly every day. Can you imagine the angst, guilt, and emotional emptiness inside of a parent who needs to make that decision? It's another case of having to make a best decision based on two less-than-optimal choices. Be aware that these decisional thoughts are normal, and if you need to talk to someone, do so. There are many choices here; spouse, friend, therapist, and in my case, I highly recommend the latter.

I love people and light up when in a social gathering, but there are some days when I'm done with humans. I'm sure many of you feel this way too. It's normal behavior, and I also can be a bit of a loner from time to time. It's in this environment that I find the best therapy for me is to write. I'll share these writings with the people I love, and it works for me. I also hope that it is of benefit to that person as well.

Find your "mojo" and do that. Maybe it's going for a long drive, maybe it's having a good cry, maybe it's blasting music (another of my favorites). Whatever; if it works for you and doesn't harm anyone else, give yourself that peace. You deserve that. *Caring of self is not selfish.* With a storyline in our lives about the relative lack of control, this is one area we absolutely can control. Take care of yourself, always.

How about those deep dark secrets no one like to think about, the inescapable and incomprehensible fact that there are deviant people out there who will take advantage of your child. These types of people are found in the public and in families, maybe even your own. It's not a pleasant thought, but one that we must be aware of in order to make good decisions for our adults. *Caretakers are vigilant and suspicious for their child.*

Look past the familial boundaries; ask who some of these people you would trust with your adult hang out with, what is their job history, what does their social media account look like? Pay for a background check; it's your adult we're talking about here. Be as honest and objective as an employer would be when hiring for a position. After all, it's only the most important job in the world from your perspective.

I have a personality trait that tends to see the best in people, so the traditional rose-colored glasses I often wear need to be thrown in the garbage can for this exercise. Be extremely aware and hyper-vigilant about who your adult is associating with, especially when they're alone; you are their voice and their reasoning agent, so own it! *Caretakers need to be vigilant.*

Here are some guidelines to assist, and remember a key point here is that the ask is easier than the acceptance. You may have to modify what you had in mind for your disabled adult's care after you pass, and procrastination does not equal love.

I have a couple of friends in mind who I could ask but I won't. One is a great guy, no children of his own, and lives an hour away. The second one is a great guy, nearly seventy, and due to a divorce will probably have to work for quite a while to get back on track. I love them both dearly, and they are the friends I could call at three in the morning for anything. Anything that is, except this. It wouldn't be fair to them, to me, or to Derek. My parents are both deceased, and my only sibling lives in Florida, twelve hundred miles away.

This leaves me with two other options: my children. My oldest child doesn't want kids of his own, and my daughter is not yet married and not sure of her desire to have kids either. It's hard to expect people who have no kids to care for a person with a disability. It's harder still to expect them to give up their lives, their liberty, to live a life that is foreign to them and care for a person who isn't theirs. I love my children to the extent that I would not place this burden upon them.

In hard decisions, I try to place myself in the other person's shoes and see issues through their lens. I've thought about this long and hard, and it is unrealistic and unfair to ask another person to give up so much. You may find that person, and I hope you do, but don't count on it, as I bet the odds are less than one in a hundred that anyone would accept the task. The best solution is the one that does the least harm to your disabled adult.

Considerations for finding your own solution. Be aware of your own situation and run some parallels to this solution, take some ideas from it and change them a bit, tweak them, whatever it takes to fit your situation. Our son is as unique as your disabled adult is. Identify their traits both positive and negative that will impact your decision making. Make a list of the most important traits top to bottom; it's that simple.

Align these traits of your adult's needs with what you have at your disposal. Do you own your own home, do you have a nurse in the family, what does your bank account look like? Be object-ive in your thoughts; do not grade your disabled person with any preconceived notions. *Be objective*; see him for what he truly is. Is he a large person (harder to handle physically), does he have medical needs that are extraordinary (IVs, wheelchair), does he have prescription needs that are extraordinary? What are his likes and dislikes? Exactly what can he accomplish on his own versus in a group setting? Does he get along well with others? What are his food allergies? The more accurate picture you can paint the better off your child/adult will be.

Once your analysis is done, have a conversation with your spouse or the other parent, as this decision has to be made together. Try to understand that this is a conversation between two adults, often the same two that brought this child into the world, and you'll get better results. In this example, having a parent/non-spouse can be beneficial as they will often see things from a different perspective.

Embrace these differences and don't be so quick to dismiss them. Always assume positive intent. With these traits and obstacles in mind, start to formulate a plan that will make the best sense for your adult when you are not here. In these difficult moments when speaking with a parent who isn't in the same household, please try to stay calm and slow down. A marriage can be stressful enough without a disabled child;

adding a dislocated parent to the mix when making life-altering decisions will be hard at best. Try to keep decency and decorum in your conversations.

Think of is this way: Would you talk to your adult in a disparaging manner? Of course you wouldn't, so don't do it when conversing with your co-parent. You both had a hand in producing this child, and you ought to have enough love in your hearts to get past the differences you had with each other and leave them in the past. *Caretakers do what is best for their child.*

Here is one solution that my wife thought of for our situation from her observations: We live in a three-bedroom ranch house; all the bedrooms are in the same side of the house next to the bathroom and the kitchen. We have a living space adjacent to the kitchen. This is where Derek has lived his entire life. He is autistic; this part of our decision making was the easiest precisely because one of his major disabilities is autism.

He is used to this place, and his behavior would probably change dramatically for the worse if he moved. His first and most pressing issue has now been solved. Derek's next major issues are his medications. He takes a lot of them and at multiple times daily, so we need someone to administer them. We will accomplish this by having his aide dispense his medications according to his needs and her schedule. For instance, if he needs to take Med A 1x daily, she will administer it; if they are needed 2x daily, one of those times she will administer them. The meds at night can be given by another caretaker or family member.

His safety is top of mind and luckily for us, our house is paid off and would probably require only about $12-15,000 budget annually to run on. This should take care of taxes, insurance, and all utilities, with some left over for repairs and maintenance. The last primary piece of Derek's post-parent life is to find two tenants to occupy the other two bedrooms at a nominal rent of $500 monthly, exceptionally inexpensive where I live.

The hard-and-fast requirement is that someone is here at night with Derek for safety reasons. If there's a fire, if he needs medical attention, someone can call and get assistance immediately. We think it's a good plan and one that fits our specific, unique set of circumstances and which addresses Derek's most important liabilities. If you can follow the outline of identifying your adult's needs and wants and categorize them according to importance, e.g., safety, life-threatening issues, medication, etc., your particular game plan will start to form.

Be honest. The old axiom of garbage in, garbage out in a data set when making a decision has never been truer. The more pertinent data you have at your disposal, the better the decisions you will make for your disabled adult. Remember that the decisions you make now will impact their life well after you've passed on, so be smart about them and give them the attention they deserve.

Let's go back to the support groups I spoke of earlier. This road we've all traveled down is lonely, difficult, and more often than not, unrewarding. We may find ourselves down in the dumps and not in the best of moods when discussing these topics. It's okay to be human.

Although you've spoken with doctors, aides, therapists, your mother, your friends, Joe from Facebook, and others to get as much information as you can, you will have missed more than you amassed.

There is a wealth of information out there, and it's always changing. Seek out your support groups and the bank of knowledge they collectively hold. It's not that any single person is smarter than you, but I guarantee the whole group knows more than you by a factor of at least ten. They've lived nearly the same life as you from forty thousand feet, but when you get down to the ground level and into the details, you'll find a massive amount of valuable intel that you can use to your advantage and your disabled child's advantage too.

Here's why. They've gone down rabbit holes you didn't even know existed and have come up with solutions based on their findings. They have dozens of people they have shared their experience with, and those people have offered advice, some wrong, some spot on. It's okay to use this experience to find the best life for your child and yourself.

The game changes all the time. I'll tell you from personal experience that when my mother was in a nursing home in Florida in the late 1990s, the government went back two years on any money that might have been misappropriated. For instance, if the nursing home resident had given a gift of money or assets to her children in the previous two years or less, it would be investigated. If it was found to be fraudulent, the money was returned to the nursing home resident and then to the nursing home. That same rule has now been extended to five years in a lookback provision instituted in 2006. Had this rule been in effect and not known about by a caretaker for a disabled adult, the results could have been devastating financially.

It is your fiduciary responsibility to know the laws and how they affect you and your child/adult. This means you must own this piece of business by knowing every law, bill, change, and nuance to every item that may affect your disabled person's eligibility for grants, retirement funds, and any other plan they may qualify for.

It's okay if you don't have the time; find a lawyer who special-izes in disability law. Seek out your support group once more for advice and any past experiences they may have had with a given lawyer and proceed with caution. Your disabled person deserves this type of thoroughness. I will speak to this in greater detail in a couple of chapters.

Do not be afraid to ask for assistance. It can be difficult, as the mindset we've all had in our epic travels thus far has been one of "I'll figure it out. I'll get it done." You probably can, but a better and less-stressful way may be to hire people who know more than you. It will be money well spent. Ever hear the saying, "pay peanuts, get monkeys" in your travels? Hiring a professional is often the best way to go.

I read this little saying quite some time ago: "Some people aren't good at asking for help because they're so used to being the 'helper.' Throughout their life they've experienced an unbalanced give and take, so their instinct is usually, 'I'll figure it out on my own.' The self-reliance is all they've ever known." Does this sound like someone you know? The world has given you a heavy burden to carry; it's okay to share this burden with professionals and your friends and family.

My final thoughts on this discussion are simple: Do what is right for your adult. Leave the best opportunity for a life that can be well-lived long after you have departed this earth. Provide the necessary tools for your adult and for their caretakers. Speak from the grave. Your legacy should be centered on "Did I do the best for my adult?" Did I have the foresight to balance short- and long-term goals for my adult?

One of the best things you can do is to spread the responsibilities to multiple people, so that no one is overwhelmed and so there are checks and balances among them. Try to assign Powers of Attorney to different folks you can trust (might not be family members) and who are willing to help. These include durable/financial, medical, and others. I'll provide a link in the last chapter clarifying each.

In my journey with Derek, I've learned so much about life. I have changed materially who I am and what I stand for in multiple disciplines. Who I was as a teenager or a person in my twenties seems very long ago. As I look back on my development of self, one thing stands clear: I would not be the person I am today without the benefit of knowing the dynamic of a special needs child and family.

There have been major life hurdles to cross and disappointments blacker than ink at the bottom of the Marianas Trench. There were despondent feelings of hopelessness and sadness, and a general malaise that hovered over me like a Golden Gate fog. It was not I that overcame these feelings alone; it was a collective effort by my family that helped me to overcome these hardships and be the person I am today.

There could not be enough "thank you's" in this lifetime to my wife from me. Our story of nearly thirty-two years has been filled with happiness and optimism because of her inner spirit. She belongs in the Olympics of Wife and Mother, standing proudly on the podium where she should reside for eternity. To my son, the little man, D, Mr. D, Mr. Guy, and finally by his name on his birth certificate, Derek, I love you. Thank you for taking us on this journey and thanks for fighting like you do. You are special in so many ways, and our family loves you for it.

Here's why we should give thanks to our special needs bundles of joy; they've taken us places we never knew we could go, conquered obstacles we never knew existed, and came out the other side better off for it. Our lives have been enriched by the patience, love, and empathy we've displayed on our journey together. They have made us better humans. If you're honest with yourself, you'll recognize a pre- and post-person in your own journey.

The pre-human took events for granted, thought we deserved a great life just for living, and had limited empathy for others. Our and hopefully your post life looks much different; we have empathy for just about everybody, we take nothing for granted, and we earn our keep and are grateful for each tidbit of good fortune we receive. We treat others with respect, and we'd like to think this rubs off on those folks we treat well so they may do the same to the people they socialize with. Call it the pebble and the ripple-in-the-pond effect, and I'd be okay with that. Be the contagious spirit that infects others positively.

Chapter 18

Finance for Caretakers and Disabled Adults

A visit with a financial advisor is one of the best gifts you can give yourself and your disabled adult. Retirement planning and end-of-life planning are difficult in a normal setting. Retirement calls for funds that are meant for you to draw interest on to live out your remaining days in relative comfort. I urge all of you to at least go online and get familiar with any number of financial tools such as retirement calculators. (Provided in the reference chapter 21)

These tools can give you a great estimate of what funds you will need for any number of scenarios that you can plug in. If you're reading this and your adult just graduated, you're probably in your forties, and you should have done this already. If not, get started immediately on a plan for your future, a future that now includes ensuring your disabled adult gets to live to the best of their ability.

Here's one of the very best illustrations that finance professionals use in their daily interactions: **The Rule of 72.** The rule states that an amount of money will roughly double in the number of years it takes a specific interest rate earned and divide that number into the number seventy-two.

Here's an example. If you have $10,000 in an investment account and the interest rate is 8%, your money will double every nine years (72/9 = 8%). Your original investment of $10,000 is now $20,000 after the nine-year timeframe. Let's play along, shall we? Take a responsible adult, one who starts planning for his retirement in his early twenties, fresh out of college. He starts with $10,000 in an IRA at the age of twenty-four. At the age of sixty-nine, Mr. Responsibility will have about

$320,000 in his retirement account without adding another dime of his own money.

Let's take his brother. Mr. Ir (as in irresponsibility) takes his time finding his way through life and starts just nine years later at his age of thirty-three. Guess how much starting nine years later will cost him? If you guessed about $160,000 you get the gold star for the day. Here's the math:

Age 24 $10,000

Age 33 $20,000

Age 42 $40,000

Age 51 $80,000

Age 60 $160,000

Age 69 $320,000

The reason I chose 8% as a return is that is an average of what you could expect to receive over the course of forty-five years in a stock market investment. This example showcases how important it is to start early rather than by trying to play catch-up in the back half of your life. Remember, it's not just you who is the beneficiary here; it's your spouse, your family, and ultimately your disabled adult.

I'll give you my personal example to help. I was always a business owner until the age of forty-two when I sold my business to the company that would employ me from that point on. They paid me a tidy sum for my business, and I locked myself in one of our bedrooms in our home and researched retirement funds like I was rabid. I had this passion to find out where I could best invest my money.

I learned more in those two weeks than in any class I ever took at school. I set up my own retirement fund, confident that I had done my due diligence for myself and my family. One of the primary reasons I sold my business was my health; I had back surgery when I was thirty-four, and delivering cases of Tropicana juice in glass bottles wasn't going to make my back any healthier. The second reason was this company that now employed me offered a pension and a 401k plan. I knew I had made the right move for all involved, I could finish my career with my health, and I would be able to retire with the necessary funds to support my family.

Let me provide another example of discipline in my retirement planning; the money I received for my business was substantial and I used just about all of it for seed money for retirement. The only money I didn't invest was the money I used when I took Laurie out to dinner to celebrate.

Another wise strategy is putting any pay raise you may receive towards building your nest egg. I did this and in a fluke year, I was lucky enough to get a really good raise, was promoted, and received a great bonus. I placed my entire raise into my 401k and paid tuition for my daughter's school with my bonus. The promotion basically covered any living expenses I would have for years to come. My rationale was if I lived on the money I made before I received the promotion, I should be able to live on the extra for a long time, and I have. Discipline in the financial department when I was young will no doubt help me and my family enjoy a decent retirement. I hope the following explanations assist you in making great choices for you and our family.

Financial products number in the hundreds, and you would do well to educate yourself about the most popular options. In a theme that runs through our world, there is no one-size-fits-all strategy. The basic players include 401ks, IRAs, SS, and pensions.

The easiest way to gain financial independence is to get started. Sounds so simple, doesn't it? It's not. As pensions have gone the way of dinosaurs, companies have moved to offering 401ks for their employees. It's been a slow-go for most people to realize that they are responsible for their financial future. It's not the government's, it's not the company's, and it's not your parents' responsibility; it's yours, plain and simple.

The 401k is the most logical place to start and the easiest. Payroll deductions are easy to set up, and the financial pro tip of all times is that if your company offers a match and most do, start with maximizing that match. Example: If you earn $60,000 a year and your company offers a match of 50% up to 4% of your pay (2%), the least amount you should be contributing is 4% or $2,400 annually. The company match is 2% or $1,200. This is *FREE* money that will compound every year and build savings for you and your adult if they are your beneficiary.

I wholly understand that money may be tight for us in caretaker land, but find a way to accomplish this basic goal. Look at it this way: If you don't contribute the maximum that the company matches, you're throwing away $1,200 every single year; when you tack on the interest you aren't compounding, it becomes a huge financial mistake. By the way, this is a very conservative example I've given here as many companies offer more generous plans.

IRAs work very much like 401ks with a difference; there are no added contributions from a company. In most applications, they are used by folks who have no access to a company plan or by folks who own their own business. Just like a 401k, they can build in value over time and become a vital tool in planning for the future. In both 401k and IRA funds, there are two types to invest in: traditional and Roth.

It's important to know the difference between the two as it can cost you money in retirement if you choose poorly. Traditional plans dictate the funds used for either are given a tax break when the investment is made; the funds grow tax-free until it's time to take them out. This benefits most folks, as many people start out life in a lower tax bracket and they don't invest much money as they are saving for a car, a house, and all the items one must buy when starting out life.

As we progress through life, we make more money, invest more, and usually find ourselves in a higher tax bracket. This benefit is best described in the following example. If you're able to invest $4,000 annually while in the 15% tax bracket while in your twenties, the taxes not paid amount to $600 a year. Do the math in your forties when you are able to save $10,000 annually in the 28% tax bracket and the savings increase to $2,800 a year. When retirement beckons, most people fall back into a much lower tax bracket; let's use 15%. When this retirement money is taken out, your tax on $10,000 will be $1,500. You can see the benefit from investing heavily in your forties at a 28% tax rate amounts to $1,300 (28-15=13%) on every $10,000 invested.

Both of these investment vehicles have maximum contribution amounts; in a 401k, the max as of 2020 is $19,500, and in an IRA it is $6,000. The good news on each plan is that you have a catch-up contribution of $6,500 in a 401k and $1,000 in an IRA if you are over the age of fifty. If you own your own business, there are Simple IRAs as well, and it is best to speak to a financial advisor on how to set these up as there are many more variables to talk through. I have included a link to the IRS guidelines about this in the reference chapter (21).

Yet another option on retirement savings is called a Roth and can be either a 401k or IRA instrument. The Roth is still funda-mentally contributed to just like a traditional 401k/IRA, except that there is zero tax break given at the time of contribution. It can still come out of your paycheck just like the traditional retirement savings accounts, and it will still build for you through your contributing years. One of the biggest differences is when you start to take money out of your Roth, there is no taxation. Simply put, the government gave you no tax break at time of contribution; you will not be required to pay any taxes upon withdrawal. There is a stipulation where you cannot touch the previous rolling five years of contributions.

For instance, if you retire at sixty-five, any monies placed into the Roth IRA from age sixty on cannot be withdrawn tax-free. This is a rolling five-year period. There are exceptions to this rule, but in general you will be subject to a 10% penalty. Exceptions include but are not limited to: if you yourself have become totally or permanently disabled or if the funds are to be used as a first-time homebuyer.

Additionally, you will be required to claim this amount of money as earnings in the year you withdrew it. This penalty was designed to be severe to discourage workers from using retirement funds for anything but just that. I would highly recommend leaving retirement funds in place until you actually retire. If you need short-term borrowing for an emergency, there are many other avenues to pursue that are less costly.

Social Security. One of the biggest decision you will have to make in your life is when to take SS. The phantom date you will die is the correct answer to solving this problem. Unless you know something I don't, nobody knows when they will leave this earth.

Here's the issue. SS can be taken as early as age sixty-two and as late as age seventy as of 2020. The median age for our purposes will be sixty-five. If you elect to take SS at that age, you will enjoy a paycheck of X amount every month courtesy of the contributions both you and your employer have made.

The top thirty-five years of employment income are used to help calculate your benefit. The benefit grows greater near the end of your working life in most cases, because you are at your highest earnings in your career. It's important to understand this as most folks earn next to nothing in their age twenty-three or below years.

After college graduation is when most folks start to see their earnings ramp up. Gone are the days when you are studying for your third final in as many days while working for $10 an hour at the pizza shop while enjoying the college experience. An example would be if you earn $15,000 in the year before you graduate at twenty-one and you earn $60,000 at age twenty-three at your new job, providing you have at least thirty-five years of qualified earnings history, the $15,000 year-twenty-one wages disappear from the calculation. I will tell you not to retire too early or too late. *The problem is nobody knows when they will die.*

Using the age of sixty-five in the above example, for every year you work past this age and for every year you retire before this age, your benefits will be affected roughly 8%. Let's say you've done a good job throughout your career, earning pretty good wages and not being unemployed for any long stretches. You may qualify for a monthly benefit of $2,400 at age sixty-five. If you elect to retire at sixty-two, your benefits will be reduced by roughly 24%; conversely, if you retire at seventy, they will be increased by roughly 40%!

If you do the math, it's a vast difference either way; your monthly benefits will now be approximately $1,824 if you retire early at sixty-two and approximately $3,360 if you retire at seventy! It's alluring to wait until age seventy to retire as the monthly dollar change is about $1,500 or $18,000 annually, but that death date looms large in your decision making.

Let's play a morbid game; let's say you die at seventy-five from an unforeseen issue and had elected to work until seventy to get the largest benefit. You would have collected $201,600, not including COLAs (cost of living adjustments). Sounds pretty good, doesn't it?

Let's use the same example but instead of retiring at seventy, you decided sixty-two was the best option. You would have collected $284,544! If you retired at sixty-five, it would be $240,000. The difference is in the number of months extra you were able to collect. In the example of retiring at sixty-two versus seventy, there would be 96 extra months of payments coming in before you collected a penny if you retired at seventy.

Compounding this decision even more is that in the disabled family dynamic there is usually a huge disparity in income produced by one spouse over the other. The primary caretaker will usually not work a high-paying job, and in all actuality may not even qualify for SS benefits as the minimum is forty quarters of full-time earning or ten years' worth. My spouse is in that cohort.

Meanwhile, the non-primary caretaking spouse will earn a much better salary and qualify for a better benefit. Why is this important? While we're on the subject of death, a surviving spouse can elect to take either her own SS payment or her spouse's, whichever is greater. It is a large factor in deciding when to retire. Remember when I implored you not be unselfish? This is one of those examples. The primary wage earner in most cases will probably want to work until a max benefit is realized. It's not only for his benefit to max out; it's for the security of his spouse and family and his disabled adult.

Is your head spinning yet? There are so many variables and so many unique situations that occur in an individual family that there can be no correct answer to the absolute age of retirement. How about quality of life, how about paying your penance so you can live the life you've imagined, how about...grab a piece of paper, log on to your computer, get yourself a calculator, put on a pot of coffee, and hash it out with your spouse. It's another in yet a long line of important decisions you must make as a caretaker.

Here is a benefit I uncovered while reading through the Social Security website. It's called the Family Maximum Benefit and paraphrasing, it allows a family that meets the criteria to collect as much as $4,000 in a monthly benefit. Here's how: The qualifiers include a family with a member who was disabled before the age of twenty-one and one of the two parents has to be the primary caretaker.

The caretaker and the disabled child/adult can each collect 50% on the primary wage earner's monthly benefit. In a situation where the wage earner is receiving a $2,000 monthly SS benefit, the caretaker and disabled person each receive 50% or $1,000 monthly. In this case, the monthly max has been achieved, and if it occurs at age sixty-four, for instance, it may not make sense to continue to earn. Retirement is certainly an option.

Something to think about as a caution is "what happens if the primary wage earner dies soon after retiring?" The family monthly max no longer applies, and the fallback position is that the surviving spouse will receive her husband's check of $2,000 and the disabled adult will reapply for SSI benefits, currently around $700 monthly. That's a big difference of $1,300 monthly or $15,600 annually ($4,000-2,700). A case could be made to work until a $2,500 monthly benefit is realized and adding the $700 SSI benefit, a $3,200 monthly benefit is now received. It's still less than the $4,000 but maybe a better compromise.

Pensions are nearly totally phased out in the business world as 401ks have become the vehicle of choice for retirement money. Company pensions are expensive to fund and maintain, and they're a drag on the company and its bottom line. There is one benefit to a company pension that I'd like to explain, though; if your company has a lump sum distribution available, I would strongly suggest taking that option rather than the monthly payment. Here's why. If you should die shortly after receiving your monthly payment and you're not married, tough luck for your disabled adult, who will not receive anything.

If you are married and you chose to have your monthly distribution paid out to you 100%, your spouse and your adult lose. They will again receive nothing. If you chose a 50/50 distribution, your monthly payment initially will be lower and upon your death your spouse will receive the same payment. Both of these options could potentially leave a vast amount of money that is uncollectable. You worked at a company for a long time to receive these benefits, so why not maximize the monetary value?

The lump sum payment should be taken, as this is guaranteed money that you can then place as a rollover into an IRA; it doesn't matter if you die the next day, because your spouse and your child will have it for eternity. Your death is not the best option for you, but you have done what is best for the family financially. As always, I would recommend speaking with a financial advisor as everyone has a different situation.

Life Insurance policies are another financial tool to assist with retirement. One of the basic questions you should consider as a caretaker is whose life is more valuable strictly from a financial replacement value. I earn a good living, and my replacement life insurance policy should cover my earnings enough so that my family could live without my income.

However, my wife, who does not earn, is potentially more valuable to our family than I am. If she were to die, I would lose my income as who would then care for Derek? My loss of income is compounded by the fifty or so jobs she does at home that I would now have to do. From being a chauffeur, hair-dresser, cook, maid, and the other jobs she does, I'd be the one that either must pay someone to do these jobs, or do them myself. It's an interesting dilemma and one that each caretaker should acknowledge.

Special Needs Trusts are a must-have in your financial toolbox. Think of these as a placeholder for your special needs recipient, and any money that is deposited in these accounts will not disqualify him from SSI. The limit on assets owned by a person collecting an SSI account is $2,000 as of 2020. There are three main types of SNTs: first-party, third-party, and a pooled trust.

Often in family inheritance situations, a sum of cash is left to a disabled person and that inheritance, if larger than $2,000 and not placed in a trust, will trigger the SSI payment to stop. Remember, $2,000 is the maximum cap on assets if you are collecting SSDI. This may be the most important financial decision you can make for your disabled adult. What good is an inheritance received if it triggers a stop payment of your adult's only means of income?

First-party trusts do exactly what I just mentioned; they hold money in an account from an inheritance or in another common example, from an accident that may have caused the disability in the first place. It's unfortunate that these large settlements, if left unprotected by a trust, can trigger the stop payment for SSI, but you now have an answer for protection of assets for your disabled person. There is a serious caveat that must be considered when establishing a first-party trust, though; when the beneficiary, your adult in this case, dies, any remaining assets in the trust will be turned over to the government for any reimbursements incurred by Medicaid. Think of this as payback to the government for the large expense of caring for a disabled person.

Third-party trusts work a little differently, in that other folks can contribute to your special needs adult's account. Think of the trust as a placeholder for your disabled adult that _other people_, mostly family members, will contribute to for your adult's benefit. Many different assets can be used to help build this trust such as real estate, stocks and bonds, or cash. The biggest change from a first-party is that any funds left after the beneficiary dies do not have to be paid back to the government for Medicaid reimbursement. The main reason for this is these funds were never technically the disabled adult's; they were placed there by others for financial assistance.

Pooled trusts are very complex and involve multiple disabled persons, and my advice on any of these trusts is to consult a trusted lawyer to find the best fit for you and your adult. As caretakers, we have the responsibility to do what is right for our disabled adult and not ourselves. The financial world and especially end-of-life discussions can be some of the most emotional conversations we ever have in our lives. Do not make any rash decisions based on raw emotion.

If you feel pressured to make a decision, stop the conversation immediately; tell counsel you feel this way, and walk away if need be. It's a sad reality that there is much money to be made in this field, and there are those who will take advantage of you for their financial gain. The way I look at it is you have two people on your side: yourself and your disabled adult. Fight for them just as hard as or even harder than you would for yourself.

Managing these first-party trusts can become a game of cat-and-mouse to utilize the funds in the best way for your adult, as you don't want to leave any more dollars in the account than reasonable given the fact that what is left will essentially be lost to the government. In a perfect world, you would draw the last dollar out of the account for your adult on the day they pass. Not a nice thought to have, but one to be cognizant of finan-cially. These financial decisions are complex, and it's up to you to understand them in a way that best benefits your adult. They are depending on you, so be the best advocate for them by understanding and making the best decision based upon available information.

ABLE accounts are named after a 2014 law passed by Congress and stand for <u>Achieving a Better Life Experience Act</u>. These accounts provide for additional funds to be used by the disabled adult without defaulting on SSI payments. The $2,000 limit on assets is absurdly low for these folks, and I have to give a shout out to my Congressman from RI, Mr. James Langevin, founder and co-chair of the Bipartisan Disabilities Caucus, for his role in passing this bill.

I met Mr. Langevin at an Autism Walk at Goddard Park in Warwick, RI, circa April 2011 and specifically asked him about what types of funds might be available for disabled adults to save money in tax-free accounts, much like our own retirement accounts.

Congressman Langevin, who is disabled himself, assured me that things were in the works and that he would have an aide call me to discuss any ideas I had. We met on a Sunday, and the following day around noon I received a call from one of his aides. I really thought it was one of my friends pranking me, but no: It was the real deal alright. I specifically remember where I was at the time of that call; I was driving a large truck in Norton and I pulled over so I could hear his associate speak.

We discussed many of the things Mr. Langevin and I discussed and what's important here is the immediate follow-up by the Congressman. It's this type of tenacity we all must have as caretakers. As caretakers, we know the struggle and the hardships we all must endure, and Mr. Langevin, being an advocate for disabled folks while being disabled himself, speaks to his credibility about these issues.

An ABLE account is not yet available in all fifty states, but as of 2020, forty-one states are participating in this program. There's good news for folks in those states who have not set theirs up yet, though: Many other states allow for out-of-state residents to partner with their states to allow for a fund subject to that state's rules. The yearly contribution from all sources is $15,000. The lifetime cap is $100,000 in accounts for folks receiving SSI/SSDI and $300,000 for folks not receiving Social Security. A disability is recognized under these guidelines as one that is expected to last for more than one year and was diagnosed before the age of twenty-six.

The rules and regulations vary widely among states, and homework must be done to ensure the best return for your adult. Some states have higher maintenance fees on their funds; some offer tax breaks if they live in the same state where they invest their dollars.

Some states exclude other states from utilizing their state's programs, and others have prevented Medicaid from accessing what is in an ABLE fund after the recipient's death (much like special needs trusts). For example, Wisconsin does not have an ABLE account set up as of this writing, but as a resident, you are able to access all of the other states' programs that allow ABLE access from a state other than their own. Currently there are twenty-eight states that allow this. These are changing at a rapid pace, and I suggest if you want up-to-date information, visit your state's ABLE account website for decision making purposes.

Chapter 19

Self-Care

"To thine own self be true."

William Shakespeare

If you've ever had that day where you were spit on, thrown up on, had feces smeared upon your furniture, or been called names you wouldn't call your worst enemy, welcome to the club. If you'd like to take a shower after reading that last line, go right ahead; I'll be here when you get back. Our disabled children and adults can be guilty of testing us like no other human on the planet.

Still, we love them more than any other human on the planet. Just when we think we've reached our breaking point, boom; something else happens that pushes the envelope. How many times have we heard, "Honey, you'll never guess what junior did today?" and the stock response "No way!" Just when you thought it couldn't get any worse...here's how to make it better.

Humor. Humor works. If you don't have this skill naturally, better order some from Amazon; just click add to cart and you'll be all set. Otherwise, you'll be in for a long day and life if you can't find a silver lining in the next episode of "You've got to be kidding me." Of course, this episode is brought to you by the love of your life. It's hard when you're having that day described above, to take a step away and laugh. I've been there; we all have as caretakers. We must always remember to keep our wits about us, and if we can't find humor in the moment, laugh about it later. Lighten the mood for your spouse if you can with a silly moment from the past that only you two would understand. Make that funny face or gesture, support her with a hug, and then pinch her butt. Be aware of the moment, lighten it up, and try to make it better for all.

Here's my example. Derek had just been dressed for bed and he was a little off that evening, but nothing serious. We had just administered meds and were ready to settle down until bedtime for him. He decided that whatever he ate for dinner he would show us again, all over the couch that we just replaced with new coverings and sheets, and all over his pajamas too. I remember this evening very well, as both Laurie and I were exhausted from the day's activities and were waiting to enjoy some sleep. First reaction was "Are you kidding me?" I'm sure there was an expletive or six thrown in there by me.

Choreographers around the country should have been there to videotape what we did. I immediately started to undress Derek, Laurie was already wetting down the towels to clean him up, and getting his new PJs. I cleaned him up, and threw the wonderful-smelling mess of bedsheets, couch covering, and pajamas in the washing machine.

By the time I walked back upstairs, Laurie had dressed him, and I started brushing his teeth as Laurie had already brought out his toothbrush. We laid new bedding down on the couch, and the whole episode was done in ten minutes tops. We were a well-oiled machine; she did what I didn't, the job got done, and Derek was okay the rest of the night.

I don't remember what I said, but I know I made Laurie laugh; she was an easy target being so tired. It's sometimes hard to believe when in a moment like that, but still millions of people around the globe had it worse than you during that time, and still will long after you've recovered from your episode. *Be grateful always.*

Close your eyes for a minute and dream of the things that make you happy. Write that list down, put your name on it, and next to your name write the following down: I will take care of myself by doing at least one of these things weekly. This is your list, your getaway money, your Cherries Jubilee after that ribeye dinner you crave so much.

Your list should include something physical, something mental, and something you don't need anybody else for. Meditation works for many folks as do puzzle books or a hike in the woods. Make that pact and promise yourself you'll practice this self-care. *Caretakers care for themselves too.*

This me time is the most selfish thing you will ever do in your caretaker life. It will recharge your batteries and spark your self interest in whatever activity you choose. It will redirect your mind to a place that you enjoy. Your brain will train you to anticipate these activities that you love, so that you will have something wonderful in your life to enjoy. Just you and your activity; nobody else. Be blissful, be ignorant, be calm, and be lost in these moments. It is the very core of self-care. Yoga, meditation, exercise...whatever takes you away from the high-stress madness we all manage every day is your go-to place.

Oddly enough, being selfish in this way will actually help the caretaker/spouse/disabled adult relationship. Ever wonder why there are a handful of elite athletes who rise to the top in the toughest situations? It's because they've found a way to focus their best efforts at the most clutch time. They can do this as they have found an inner peace that lets them block out every-thing else at the moment and concentrate on the task at hand. Sound like anybody we know?

It's us; we have to focus our best efforts when the time is most crucial for our children. These critical snapshots are where we need to perform as elite caretakers. These moments require so much psychological demand, physical dexterity, and mental toughness that we need a release. We deserve a release, which is exactly why we need to audit our self-care from time to time.

Ask yourself why you are feeling a little more down than usual; I'll bet it's because you haven't been in self-care mode enough. Those endorphins in your body and you need to be reacquainted. If you can't remember the last time you performed self-care, it's probably time to do it. If at all possible, and it can be tricky given our lifestyle, keep a schedule for *your* time. It should be as routine as eating breakfast or getting dressed in the morning.

My wife has her Saturday getaways with her girlfriends. It usually involves four or five friends, and when not all of them can make it, she still makes it work with what's left of the group. They may not all agree on what they're doing or even when, but they eventually come to a consensus and off she goes.

It must feel good to just get away from being on the constant lookout, always on alert and aware of what situation could come up and having to be prepared for anything. It's why I'm happy she gets to enjoy this time. She always seems to have a good time and is grateful to have the time out.

For dad and Derek, it's a great time for us to spend some time together. I take him for his ride, maybe to get a shake at Dunkin', or out to the backyard. I am fully aware of the extra duties placed on me when Laurie isn't here. I'm now on high alert, ensuring all is well with his health, preparing and feeding him, dispensing meds, taking the bathroom trips, dressing him, and all those invisible duties my wife does every day that I don't see. It strengthens my love for her and for Derek and in a way, is my self-care.

I pride myself on being a caretaker in the sense that it's my job to ensure my kids get a great start in life, that I help them through their formative years, and that I'm there always for advice. I get to witness first-hand the job my wife has done with Derek and how hard and mentally exhausting it is. This just makes me more appreciative of what she does every day for Derek and for our family. Truly a win all the way around as we all enjoy a strengthened bond that continues to grow each day.

Do everything you can to make it work with your spouse. Vacations can be a real problem when living our lifestyle. Depending on the severity of the disability, some trips that are more than a week may be out of the question. Proximity from home base is another concern as being too far away from a specialized doctor could be detrimental to your child's health. *Stay positive and be flexible*.

Instead of a week's stay at a fabulous resort six hours away by plane, you could certainly pick a closer resort and make a long weekend out of it. Just go on these types of getaways a little more often. It'll give everyone something to look forward to and can reduce the stress of staying too far from home. This relative lack of stress due to being close to home will put both your and your spouse's minds at ease.

Here's how I made it work for a vacation with Laurie. I had traveled a bit for work, and one of my favorite cities I visited was San Antonio, TX. The city has a lot to offer and is completely walkable with a wonderful venue called the Riverwalk. I envisioned my wife and me visiting here when I was at my conventions for work. How nice it would be, just the two of us, cruising down the Riverwalk, visiting the Alamo, the zoo, etc. Dreaming and executing an idea are two different mindsets. When leaving a disabled child, who is fairly high-maintenance with a strict medicine regimen, without his parents requires planning. I was determined to take her there, so we formulated a plan and we came up with a solution.

We could have been negative and said, "We can't do this because we have Derek," but we *found a way* to make it work. Luckily, we have a very mature daughter who, when I asked, said absolutely, I'll watch my brother while you guys go. Have a good time. Laurie also has a girlfriend who was willing to watch Derek with Haley and provide support.

A week's stay was out of the question, so I shortened it to five days and seeing as I was familiar with the city, I could make the itinerary work for our purposes. I booked a great bed-and-breakfast, made the airline reservations, and was excited to go on a mini getaway with my wife. All the bases had been covered here and May couldn't come quick enough.

That is, until I had to solve for a physical issue. I lost a good friend during the time I made plans. We were basketball buddies from back in the day. I thought it would be a good idea to honor my friend Billy by playing basketball with another one of our friends, Brad. I'd record it and post it on Facebook. It was a beautiful day in Pawtucket, RI, and I made a move on the court I've made ten thousand times in my life. I felt what I thought was another basketball hit my calf and I collapsed. I got up and fell down again, now knowing I was hurt pretty badly.

Being the knucklehead that I am, I went to work the next day, delivering off a truck, no less, and gimped around for two days before my wife said I ought to get it checked. Do you wonder why women live longer than men? The diagnosis from the doctor was a torn Achilles. I knew I was hurt, but I did not want to let anything stop me from going to Texas. When you're age 54 and a torn Achilles impacts your health, it's a pretty severe injury and one that requires about four months of rehab.

I was leaving with Laurie in three weeks for San Antonio, and it might as well have been Tahiti for us, as we never get to go anywhere alone. I was resolute in my stance that we were still going. Laurie was not so sure.

I asked the doctor if we could wait three weeks to do the surgery, and he said no, so I asked him if I could fly safely after the operation. He stated yes with a caveat of ensuring I do exercises with my leg to keep the blood clots at bay. Easy enough, I'd be the best damn exerciser of legs the world has ever seen. My ass and my wife's ass were going to San Antonio.

Vacation day came, we packed up and, of course, I was on crutches so it was a little cumbersome, but I didn't care one bit. There is always a silver lining, remember? You get to board first when on crutches and on Southwest Airlines it's open seating. We got to sit at the front for a much better flying experience for me as the leg room was easily twice what it is from second row back. I could exercise at will and not bother anyone.

For anyone who has been on crutches for an extended period of time, you know it can be uncomfortable, especially in the heat and humidity of Texas. I never felt any pain, as the smile on my wife's face was the best elixir for pain ever made. We had a great time, and it was everything I had hoped for.

We had a great laughable moment at one of the activities I wanted to do, tubing down the Comal River. I had my surgical boot on, and they tell you to be careful as it's very slippery getting in the water. I had my back to my wife as she was closest to the water, ready to climb into the tube, and as I was taking off my boot I heard the unmistakable sound of someone falling into the water. I quickly turned around, and Laurie was nowhere to be seen. A second later, she surfaced from under the water and immediately started laughing at what she just did. Here I was, boot now off, looking at my wife saying, "What happened?" I think she missed the memo of watch out, it's slippery down there.

When times get tough for us, and they do all too often, it's good to keep these types of memories alive to fall back on. I've had a smile on my face just writing this last paragraph!

Remember that you alone are responsible for your self-care. No one knows you like you do. When it's time to destress your mind, don't wait. Another important self-care tip is to break up your self-care routine. If you find yourself doing the same thing week after week, your self-care can become inefficient. Just as you try your hardest to keep your disabled child interested in a daily function, you must do so for yourself. Life is a learning experience, and we only get one go round; make your tickets count.

Get out of your comfort zone; start a garden, buy a ten-gallon aquarium starter kit, join a book club, learn how to crochet – there are thousands of ideas to entertain. Do not limit yourself to what you've always done in the past. It will keep your brain healthy, and who knows? This new activity just might be what the doctor ordered for your child. Instead of having the bad conversation of you can't believe what Junior did today, it can become a good conversation. Maybe you find out he loves to just sit and watch fish swimming in the aquarium, or loves to play in the dirt and garden. *Successful caretakers will innovate.*

Chapter 20

The Interviews

I interviewed a cross-section of people who have ties to the world of disability as we know it. These folks are mothers, fathers, siblings, caretakers, special education teachers, social workers, and agency professionals who have graciously agreed to answer a litany of questions to help us understand our lifestyle and how to improve on it. Some of these questions were pointed and personal, and my absolute thanks go out to every person involved who took the time to answer each question from their own point of view.

The following will serve as excerpts taken from these real-life situations. I've included the questions asked, and I tried to be as thorough as possible. Some of these questions were invasive, and I want to thank every respondent for answering honestly and comprehensively. Their attention to detail and willingness to open their hearts and minds were a testament to their individual journeys.

Every single interviewee answered every question that was applicable to them. The collective thought here is that they wanted to help in any way possible, and for that I commend each of them. Our fraternity is a strong one. These folks have walked a mile in your shoes as caretakers and learning from your peers is one of the best ways to gain experience and intelligence.

I have also walked a mile in a caretaker role and felt confident going in to the interviews that their stories would mimic mine. I also felt I'd be ready and able to hear their stories and the heartache would be something I could handle. I was wrong on both counts. While each story had elements of my own, each was uniquely theirs, and their solutions, although similar, were also unique to their particular situation. The stories I heard as told by the caretaker in each instance kept my rapt attention as the emotional context was overwhelming for me to hear. .

In one instance that will stay inside my heart, a respondent replied when asked how this diagnosis has changed your life answered: "We had talked about having a family and when our first disabled child was born we had to ask ourselves what was the likelihood that we could have another like him?" In their case, the disability was genetically based and the possibility existed that any subsequent child born could not only have the same condition but the disability could be much worse.

They made the heart-wrenching decision to not have any more children. It had to be a devastating decision to come to grips with, but you'd never know it as somehow, someway, she has stayed positive throughout the years. For what it's worth, I think they made the correct decision.

There are many stories I heard that I will never forget and will serve to remind me to always be grateful, to never take life for granted, and to be thankful for all I have. We all have a bond, a responsibility to our disabled children that supersedes our own lives and to live in service to them and others who share our journey. The help we all receive, especially from these real-life interviews, should be shared within our own subset of society and also within the community that impacts our lives. The more people outside our circle who know about the struggles we encounter, the more likely they are to understand and help.

They say that the elite members of the Armed Forces, such as Seal Team Six or the Army Rangers, upon meeting one another know instantly they are part of the same unit, despite never having met before. They've gone through some intense training, they've seen things nobody else has seen, and they've survived that rigorous training with the help of others in their unit.

We've gone through some rigorous life training of our own and have seen things no other adults have seen and have survived with the help of others. We are the elite units of our own special society, and I challenge each of you to live up to that moniker. Be that person that rises to the challenge and solves for issues instead of complaining.

Please learn from these interactions and apply them towards your everyday life within the context of your disabled child/ adult's home life, social skills, eating habits, financial health, etc. Here is the list of questions:

1. How did you feel when you first received the diagnosis and what was it?
2. How did you find out about services?
3. What medicines worked/failed for you?
4. Walk me through a day in the life of.
5. What are your biggest challenges with your child?
6. What are your biggest triumphs with your child?
7. What is your go-to strategy for stress relief?
8. How have you prepared for your child's care for a future that may not include you?
9. Do you have an ABLE account, and how did you find out about it?
10. Does your child collect SSI or SSDI? EBT?
11. As a single parent, how has life changed for both you and your child?

12. What school did she attend and what services did she receive there? Was OT, PT offered and was it beneficial?
13. How could your IEP have been conducted with better results?
14. Do you use outplacement services or is your child/adult at home?
15. What in-home care do you use?
16. How do you integrate your child into a setting with the rest of the children there?
17. What is the single biggest change in your life since the diagnosis?
18. What gets you through the toughest days?
19. Have you sought out therapy to help with the stress of raising a disabled child/adult?
20. What words of wisdom would you give other people in your specific situation, i.e., the specific issue/issues of disability, single/married/divorced?

When collating this information, I learned quite a bit about our world and how impactful a positive attitude can be and how just one person or event can alter a caretaker's/disabled child/adult's day or even life! The power of positivity is alive and well. In general, I believe that these findings support my assumption that all of us are in this together, and that those who are seem to be a whole lot more helpful than those who aren't.

It's like that old saying, "The poor give more to charity because they know what it's like to be poor." We're in the trenches, we pass the ammo down the line, and we fight for each other. It's truly a community of effort, love, and unselfishness, and I'm proud to have interviewed each of these people. Thanks again to the providers of this wisdom gleaned from years of experience, from their hearts, and from their souls.

Here are some of the excerpts from my interviews:

How did you feel when you first received the diagnosis and what was it?

Almost to a person, the storyline goes like this: "I was over-whelmed." "I felt a lack of hope. I went numb." "I was scared then and what the future would hold." "My life as I knew it changed in an instant." For the interviewees this was applicable to, I was surprised at the consistency of responses. After the third interview, it seemed I was already typing what their response was going to be ahead of time. My takeaway is that we're not as different as we seem to think when faced with a grim reality. We all react nearly the same, we respond nearly the same, and we must adopt an attitude of advocacy for our children.

Walk me through a day in the life of.

This was a great question in that it elicited a variety of responses. The subset of individuals questioned included single, married, divorced, social workers, and teachers. One thought is abundantly clear: the passion for their children/students/ clients, and the love of their job. To encapsulate the responses most prevalent, we'd have to start with laughter. Laughter at the question as to "Which day am I going to have? There are so many different days!" This "I don't know what to expect" answer is at the heart of what we do as special needs parents. We are malleable, we are flexible, and we will not be deterred from making the best of every day, no matter what.

Remember to couple.

All the interviewed that had a significant other or spouse brought this up. It is a vital and elementary link to spend time with your girlfriend or boyfriend, even when married. Yes I know many of you are married yet still spend time with the person you met before you were married, the one you promised you would take care of through thick and thin, good times and bad.

Date your spouse again by bringing her flowers, taking her to that favorite spot where you two had some great memories. And if I catch you on your phone during these times when you're alone with your spouse, I swear...

This time is a gift, something to be cherished even more so than when other couples go out. It's simply because this time is of higher value to both of you. When demand is high, value goes up, Economics 101. Be that guy that gets the car door, café door, and chair for your lady. Love her like you mean it because it will strengthen the bond you both need to depend on.

Ladies, you too can play in this game. Wear the dress, perfume, and lipstick he likes best on you. Show each other you still crave this time as much as you did when you were chasing each other around all those years ago. Both of you give so much to your disabled child, it's okay; give yourself permission to spend that "give" on your significant other. You'll both be better off for it, and it will refresh your admiration for each other and when you're both happy, who else benefits? That's right, class; your child reaps the rewards of two parents who are now less stressed, filled with less anxiety, and have rekindled their love for each other, which no doubt will cascade through to the center of your universe.

Financing 101

I think financial awareness is one of the most glaring examples of how we as caretakers could do a much better job of educating ourselves. One of the findings was the inexperience of the interview cohort on financial tools available, and programs and eligibility requirements for them and their disabled child. Completely understandable given the wide variety of topics we must understand. It's one of the reasons I wrote this book; I want to educate and make available all the resources we in the disabled community can use to our benefit.

There is so much information out there today about these programs, 401k, IRA, SSI, SS, SSDI, and ABLE accounts that are available. Maybe it's because our days are filled with other more pressing issues and that we're overwhelmed Put these issues aside for now and concentrate on the financial well-being of your child. It is absolutely critical to understand the complete financial picture for you and your disabled child now and into adulthood.

Please take a few minutes to start gathering information on all of these financial tools, especially the ABLE accounts for those who qualify. There's a whole chapter dedicated to these instruments to assist and aid you in your quest to set up your disabled adult and yourself for the best future available.

Listen, no one is born a financial genius. And unless your surname is Rockefeller or Vanderbilt, you're probably going to need some financial planning. From an operational standpoint, this is the most important item to facilitate in our situation. Your adult may or may not outlive you, but don't be that person on his deathbed, saying to yourself, "I hope I did enough." *Find the time, and get it done.*

Celebrate your child's triumphs

It was a common theme through the interviews that celebrating the triumphs, no matter how small in the grand scheme of things, was so rewarding for both parent and child. My experience of watching Derek accomplish #2 (huge win for him) was echoed dozens of times by the parents. Their stories were both uplifting to me, and the way they were presented as well told it all: "It might not be a big deal to someone else," "I was so proud of my child," "It took so long, but they did it," all spoke to the pride the caretakers felt.

It's so important to celebrate these victories as much as you would for your other children, maybe even more. Everyone knows that person who never took a dance lesson, yet looks like Michael Jackson out there on the dance floor. That person should be acknowledged for their ability, but if it came rather easily, the challenge for them to succeed might be to be the best dancer of all time.

In a broader sense, we all want to achieve, and achievement can be accelerated by recognition; if you learn a new step in a process, you should be rewarded appropriately. If you develop a new process, well hey! Let's break out the champagne and balloons! If your disabled child took two months to drink out of a cup without a straw, he should get the trip to Hawaii, the Maserati, and $5,000 in spending money for his efforts. The effort was there; the prize should be commensurate with the struggle.

What is the single biggest change in your life since the diagnosis?

One of the best comments I heard was, "Being normal is so overrated." This came on the heels of her preceding sentence, which was "Life as I knew it was over." These two sentences encapsulate what we all need to do as caretakers: learn how to make lemonade. Here's a good recipe: 2 quarts of water, ¾ cup of fresh lemon juice, ½ cup of sugar. Warm slowly, mix well, add a sprig of mint, chill, and off you go.

Our stories are the epitome of living two lives, the one prior to the diagnosis and the life of a caretaker. It's the very essence of this book, learning how to embrace this lifestyle. Always keep hope front and center, and learn to manage your new life that will be different, away from normal. As my friend stated, it's overrated and she's right. Stay positive, be flexible, and adjust accordingly.

What do you do for stress relief?

There was some hesitation from most respondents on this question. The initial answer given in many cases was alcohol. My assumption is that they may have felt a certain taboo or shame over this revelation. I know many of the respondents personally, and I can tell you none of them have a drinking problem. It's a microcosm of how hard it is to give self-love; we feel guilty over a small pleasure we no doubt deserve. A martini or a couple of beers to salvage a bit of sanity hasn't hurt anyone that I know of. Don't let a feeling of guilt or shame deter you from much-needed stress relief.

Professional and Administration Learnings

There were some excellent lessons and one best practice that I'm passing on from the professionals I interviewed. I urge each of you to pass these along to your community of caretakers, schoolteachers, both regular and Special Ed, and any agencies that could implement these ideas.

The best practice that I believe could be easily instituted in nearly every school is one where a regular student sits in on a class that is normally reserved for Special Ed students. One of my respondents who teaches in a Massachusetts community reported that a regular student will mentor an SE student in a particular subject. In this case, an SE student can move from his classroom setting to an integrated setting where regular kids are taught by their teacher and there is also an SE teacher in class.

This does many wonderful things for all students. It gives the SE student a sense of camaraderie with all students and incorporates them into the whole school society. It gives them a sense of empowerment in that if they can do well in their SE class, they can follow their mentor to his classroom setting.

For the mentor, it establishes a link to a student they may never have been exposed to and creates an empathetic and inclusive bond that they too can bring back to their classroom. What a feeling it must be to mentor someone and to have them succeed based in part on how well you mentored them! For all the students in the regular classroom, it shows what one person can do to help another succeed in life.

This type of mentoring is often used in corporate America, and I've been a part of it from both ends; I've been mentored and

I've had the good fortune to mentor a couple of folks myself. I can tell you firsthand there is no greater feeling than seeing a person you've mentored have success, not only in the business climate, but in their personal life as well.

One of my success stories is a young lady who left our company, got a prestigious job at another large company, is married, and is an awesome mother of two great kids. I smile every time I think of how far she has come, and it's thanks to the people who have mentored me along the way. They paved the way for me to feel empowered, and I'm just paying it forward, which is what I hope this program's legacy becomes. *Caretakers promote lifelong learning.*

Transition from child to adult

A couple of key points I feel we all need to know occurred here in the transition space between child and adult. From an educational point of view, all caretakers should be prepared to take their child from one learning environment, which is very structured, to life. My conversations with professionals from this side of the equation were profound. Caretakers must be ready to classify their child as an adult when in adult settings. For instance, when out in public at a Target store, prompt your adult to interact with other adults of children in the store. Keep them involved in the shopping experience.

If they're able, allow them the freedom to push the carriage, place items into the carriage from a shelf, and give them an option when choosing between two types of cookies or crackers. At checkout, ask them to say hi to the cashier or others in line, and make them part of the society they have now entered as adults.

Here's why this is so important. So much work has been done at school to give them a routine, a time and place for everything that if you let this lapse, your adult may suffer withdrawal from society as a whole. That is the last thing you want for your adult. It's your job to see this comes about.

Use any method you want – a walk down a bike path, a day in the park, take them to a Little League ballgame where there are children and adults. Malls, coffee shops, even a hiking trail all work if there is trepidation about being in a closed space with others. There are enough answers for this problem; it's up to you to find the solution that works for your adult. Most of these are healthy, all are social in varying degrees, and what's the worst that can happen? Maybe get a bad cup of coffee?

What gets you through the toughest days?

Some favorites were exercising – specifically walking, hiking, some structured gym – cooking with their spouse, a hot shower, or a favorite TV show. As varied as the answers were, they all led to the same place: taking care of self. Who doesn't feel better after the isolation of a hot shower, or the feeling of when those endorphins kick-start the rest of your exercise routine? That rejuvenation and utter connection when traipsing through nature ten minutes into a hike cannot be bought in a store. Cooking affords the opportunity to be creative, when so much of our lives is structured and by the book; the end result of cooking is eating, and you have no soul if you don't enjoy that.

Self-reflection is a great practice for humans in general and a godsend for caretakers everywhere. It's important in our epic journeys to be aware of where we came from, what defines us, and how far we have come. If you could graph your life like we do in so many other disciplines, you'd plainly see how far you've come as a person, a parent, and as a caretaker.

During these activities that bring you much-needed peace, be sure to include some of your favorite moments or snapshots in life. They can be anything that brings a smile to your face, or the resurrection of a long-lost loved one who had an impact on how your personality and maybe even your life has been framed.

From a personal standpoint, I believe many of us are way too hard on ourselves, and cutting ourselves some slack is often a great remedy for a less-cluttered mind. Close your eyes in the shower and reminisce as a young man about that base hit that drove in the winning run, or when you made your momma smile as a young girl when that blueberry pie you made all by yourself was the best damn blueberry pie your dad ever ate. Open your eyes, look in the mirror, and view that smile that is now imprinted on your face, much like the memory you just relived. *Allow yourself that peace.*

Chapter 21

Reference Information

The following links will provide helpful information on a wide variety of disabilities, disorders, and medicines, all meant to educate you and start you on your quest to research all the important topics covered in this book. I have included many disability informational websites, which include the areas of disability recognized by IDEA. I have also included others that are prevalent and could happen later on in life. This is by no means a comprehensive list; rather, it's a jumping-off point to encourage further research and learning by all the caretakers who need to start somewhere. This is that somewhere.

One link that needs explanation is the one to Katie Beckett, an eligibility category in Medicaid you should know about. You can access the link that I provided on this page for RI, but for other states you'll simply have to access that specific website.

https://ripin.org/resources/katie-beckett/

I have also included links to the financial world including retirement and Social Security. I've cleared a path for all the caretakers to start; it's up to you to walk down that path and visit as many websites as you can to further your knowledge. With many publications, information can get outdated, updated, or removed because of changes in policy or law, so please keep up on your research. As always, you should contact a lawyer, finance, or health professional when making any major decision for your disabled child/adult.

Included also are links to the SIS and the IEP experiences. I highly recommend visiting these sites and saving these pages to your computer. They are invaluable when preparing for either of these important meetings with your child. Visit other sites, branch out from this information, and gather more. Continue to research as state and federal laws are always changing. If you're not sure of what you're reading and have questions, contact your city or town, school administrator, agency, support groups. Keep the information flowing and you'll find your answers. Do net get discouraged, as the volume of information is exceptionally large. If need be, take a break, practice your self-care, and get back to it when in a better frame of mind.

Caretaking includes being a great researcher.

My hope and intent when writing this book was to educate folks about special needs children, disabled adults, and the rigorous, unknown world the caretakers must navigate for them all to be successful. I was honest with my emotions, and gave some background info to show we're all alike in this fight. I included a day in the life to showcase just one couple's challenges and how we overcame them with a cocktail of positivity, flexibility, patience, and a trust in one another to do the right thing.

Interviews were conducted and the results posted to help with any questions about real-life situations outside of our home. Included with this book is a wealth of information with links to as many of the disabilities as I could think of. There is also financial advice including Social Security and ABLE account information.

Like most self-help books, I wrote this because of a need for one. I browsed a few bookstores, scoured the internet, and couldn't find one like this. I hope you all took a little something from this book. Whether it was the positive vibe, the little tidbits of how we overcame our challenges so that you could overcome yours, or helpful financial and planning info, I urge you all to share this information within your own community network of disabled folks and their caretakers. Thank you and peace be with all of you.

Sincerely, Brian Wilk

All of these links were valid as of publication.

AD/HD

https://www.healthline.com/health/adhd

https://www.cdc.gov/ncbddd/adhd/index.html

ALS (Lou Gehrig's Disease)

http://www.alsa.org/about-als/what-is-als.html

Alzheimer's Disease

https://www.mayoclinic.org/diseases-conditions/alzheimers-disease/symptoms-causes/syc-20350447

https://www.nia.nih.gov/health/what-alzheimers-disease

https://www.alz.org/help-support/i-have-alz/treatments-research

https://www.alz.org/alzheimers-dementia/facts-figures

https://www.communityresourcefinder.org/?_ga=2.87539352.1834933486.1588595341-443117355.1588595341

Autism/Asperger's

https://www.mayoclinic.org/diseases-conditions/autism-spectrum-disorder/symptoms-causes/syc-20352928

https://www.cdc.gov/ncbddd/autism/facts.html

https://www.autismspeaks.org/what-autism

https://www.ninds.nih.gov/Disorders/Patient-Caregiver-Education/Fact-Sheets/Autism-Spectrum-Disorder-Fact-Sheet

Bipolar Disease

https://www.nimh.nih.gov/health/topics/bipolar-disorder/index.shtml

https://www.healthline.com/health/bipolar-disorder

Blindness

https://health.usnews.com/conditions/eye-disease/articles/diseases-that-can-lead-to-blindness

https://lowvisionmd.org/eye-disease-that-can-lead-to-blindness/

Cerebral Palsy

https://www.mayoclinic.org/diseases-conditions/cerebral-palsy/symptoms-causes/syc-20353999

https://www.cdc.gov/ncbddd/cp/facts.html

Deafness

https://www.betterhealth.vic.gov.au/health/conditionsandtreatments/deafness-a-range-of-causes https://medbroadcast.com/condition/getcondition/hearing-loss-and-deafness

Depression

https://www.mayoclinic.org/diseases-conditions/depression/symptoms-causes/syc-20356007

https://www.psychologytoday.com/us/blog/evil-deeds/200809/is-depression-disease

Developmental Disability

https://www.cdc.gov/ncbddd/developmentaldisabilities/facts.html

https://www.ncbi.nlm.nih.gov/books/NBK223473/

Diabetes

https://medlineplus.gov/diabetes.html

https://www.diabetes.org/

https://www.cdc.gov/diabetes/basics/diabetes.html

Down Syndrome

https://www.cdc.gov/ncbddd/birthdefects/downsyndrome.html

https://www.mayoclinic.org/diseases-conditions/down-syndrome/symptoms-causes/syc-20355977

https://www.healthline.com/health/down-syndrome

Epilepsy

https://www.epilepsy.com/learn/about-epilepsy-basics/what-epilepsy

https://www.epilepsy.com/

https://www.mayoclinic.org/diseases-conditions/epilepsy/symptoms-causes/syc-20350093

Fragile X Syndrome

https://ghr.nlm.nih.gov/condition/fragile-x-syndrome

https://fragilex.org/understanding-fragile-x/fragile-x-101/

HIV/AIDS

https://www.mayoclinic.org/diseases-conditions/hiv-aids/symptoms-causes/syc-20373524

https://www.cdc.gov/hiv/basics/whatishiv.html

Multiple Sclerosis

https://www.mayoclinic.org/diseases-conditions/multiple-sclerosis/symptoms-causes/syc-20350269

https://www.nationalmssociety.org/What-is-MS

Muscular Dystrophy

https://www.mayoclinic.org/diseases-conditions/muscular-dystrophy/symptoms-causes/syc-20375388

https://www.mda.org/disease

Parkinson's Disease

https://www.mayoclinic.org/diseases-conditions/parkinsons-disease/symptoms-causes/syc-20376055

https://www.parkinson.org/Understanding-Parkinsons/What-is-Parkinsons/Stages-of-Parkinsons

PTSD

https://www.mayoclinic.org/diseases-conditions/post-traumatic-stress-disorder/symptoms-causes/syc-20355967

https://www.mdedge.com/fedprac/article/174860/mental-health/what-relation-between-ptsd-and-medical-conditions

Rett Syndrome

https://www.rettsyndrome.org/

https://www.mayoclinic.org/diseases-conditions/rett-syndrome/symptoms-causes/syc-20377227

Special Olympics

https://www.specialolympics.org/

Spina Bifida

https://www.mayoclinic.org/diseases-conditions/spina-bifida/symptoms-causes/syc-20377860

https://www.spinabifidaassociation.org/

Spinal Cord Injury

https://www.shepherd.org/patient-programs/spinal-cord-injury/about

https://www.mayoclinic.org/diseases-conditions/spinal-cord-injury/symptoms-causes/syc-20377890

Stroke

http://www.strokecenter.org/patients/about-stroke/what-is-a-stroke/

https://www.mayoclinic.org/diseases-conditions/stroke/symptoms-causes/syc-20350113

Tourette's Syndrome

https://www.mayoclinic.org/diseases-conditions/tourette-syndrome/symptoms-causes/syc-20350465

https://tourette.org/about-tourette/overview/what-is-tourette/

Traumatic Brain Injury

https://www.mayoclinic.org/diseases-conditions/traumatic-brain-injury/symptoms-causes/syc-20378557

https://emedicine.medscape.com/article/326510-overview

Katie Beckett RI

https://ripin.org/resources/katie-beckett/

Medicare/Medicaid

https://www.medicare.gov/

https://www.ssa.gov/benefits/medicare/

https://www.medicare.gov/what-medicare-covers/what-part-b-covers

https://www.medicaid.gov/

https://www.medicaid.gov/medicaid/eligibility/index.html

ADA Links

https://www.dol.gov/general/topic/disability/ada

https://adata.org/learn-about-ada

https://www2.ed.gov/about/offices/list/ocr/docs/hq9805.html

Social Security Information

https://www.usa.gov/about-social-security

https://www.foxbusiness.com/money/social-security-benefits-retirement-full-retirement-age

https://www.fool.com/retirement/2020/05/09/heres-precisely-how-social-security-spent-106-tril.aspx

https://www.google.com/search?sa=X&rlz=1C1NHXL_enUS834US834&q=social%20security%20benefit%20formula&ved=2ahUKEwiDoaWX-6bpAhXeInIEHbDvAkIQmoICKAV6BAgOEA8&biw=1366&bih=625

https://www.ssa.gov/benefits/retirement/?gclid=EAIaIQobChMI-Lusl_um6QIVhQiICR34dAi0EAAYASAAEgLr2PD_BwE

SS Family Monthly Maximum Link

https://www.ssa.gov/policy/docs/ssb/v75n3/v75n3p1.html

Financial Information

IRA/401k Retirement Guidelines 2020 link

https://www.irs.gov/taxtopics/tc557

https://www.irs.gov/newsroom/401k-contribution-limit-increases-to-19500-for-2020-catch-up-limit-rises-to-6500

https://www.forbes.com/sites/davidrae/2020/01/16/401k-for-2020/#48e45dda7903

https://money.usnews.com/money/retirement/iras/articles/ira-contribution-limits

https://www.schwab.com/ira/roth-ira/contribution-limits

SIS Information

https://www.aaidd.org/publications/supports-intensity-scale

Retirement Calculator

https://smartasset.com/retirement/retirement-calculator#MWvI9tg7dd

IEP Information

https://www.parentcenterhub.org/iep-overview/

Bibliography

Chapter 7

P. 68 Autism stats taken from www.autsimspeaks.com (April, 2020)

Chapter 12

P. 118 definition of IDEA and IEP
https://www.parentcenterhub.org/iep-overview/ (May, 2020)

P. 123 excerpt on special needs population
https://nces.ed.gov/programs/coe/indicator_cgg.asp

(April, 2020)

Chapter 15

P. 145 Supports information www.AAIDD.org (May, 2020)

Chapter 16 (May, 2020)

P. 154 stats Alzheimer's/Parkinson's
https://www.alz.org/alzheimers-dementia/facts-figures

P. 159 excerpts Mayo Clinic
https://www.mayoclinic.org/healthy-lifestyle/caregivers/in-depth/alzheimers-caregiver/art-20047577 (May, 2020)

P. 160-161 Alzheimer's financial costs
https://www.alz.org/alzheimers-dementia/facts-figures (May, 2020)

P. 160-161 Nursing home disparity
https://www.communityresourcefinder.org/?_ga=2.87539352.1834933486.1588595341-443117355.1588595341 (May, 2020)

Chapter 18

P. 182 IRS information on 401k, IRA
https://www.irs.gov/newsroom/401k-contribution-limit-increases-to-19500-for-2020-catch-up-limit-rises-to-6500 (May, 2020)

P. 183-187 SSI, SSDI, retirement info https://www.ssa.gov/ (May, 2020)

P. 188-190 Special Needs Trusts info
https://specialneedsanswers.com/what-is-a-special-needs-trust-13601 (May, 2020)

P. 190-191 ABLE account info
https://www.savingforcollege.com/529-able-accounts/ (May, 2020)

Acknowledgements

As with any large project, there are many moving parts and people who provide the ingredients for a successful outcome. It is my pleasure to acknowledge some folks who have taken this project from an idea to what you just read.

Art Stanton is the man who first seeded this endeavor by mentioning that people needed to hear my story as I was so positive about Derek's situation. This, in turn, evolved into this book and I cannot thank him enough as so many will benefit from the information inside. You're the genuine article and a friend for twenty-five years.

To my childhood friend Harry Harootunian, thank you for your insights and being one of the smartest men I've ever met. Your honesty and sincerity of opinion helped my decision making immensely. Your mom raised a good son....

As a first-time author, I was confident through the editorial process, but inexperienced with the publishing side. Enter Bill Gardner who said to me, "I have your guy." "My best man at my wedding has written five books, I'll put you two in touch." Billy is the rare breed of man you may have heard of; he does what he says he will do....

Frank Stepnowski is that man. The first time I answered the phone with Step, as he likes to be called, he opined, "How can I help you?" Step gave me indispensable information and created the title for this book. Good men are hard to come by, I've been fortunate to have these two in my life. You should check out Frank's insightful books on education. Thank you Billy and Step for all your help.

To Susan Rooks, my editor, who I desperately needed to navigate my way through the syntax, context, grammar, and punctuation, thank you for a professional outcome. I needed a captain as I was sailing in unchartered waters, and your compass was true.

To every caretaker in the land, thank you for the inspiration to write this book. We live a different life and sometimes the signposts aren't as recognizable in our world. My hope is that each reader has acknowledged a benefit (or many) from reading this book. I wish all of you Godspeed.

Most importantly, to my wife Laurie, who brought Derek into this world and has been by his side for every tear, misstep, seizure, and operation, as well as the triumphs, breakthroughs, and laughter, I love you. Thank you for what you do *every single day*. Your job is unfathomably difficult, yet every day you rise with that smile, take care of Derek with nary a complaint, and provide me with a sanctuary we call home. My life has been enriched beyond measure with you by my side. I could not do this without you, thank you, your grateful husband.

CPSIA information can be obtained
at www.ICGtesting.com
Printed in the USA
LVHW040132120820
662878LV00006B/586

9 781977 230706